WITHDRAWN

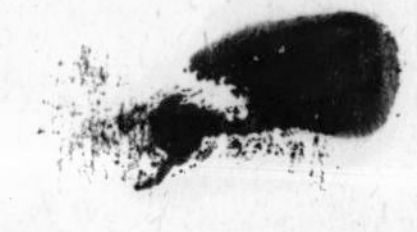

NORTH ITALIAN DRAWINGS

FROM THE COLLECTION OF THE BUDAPEST MUSEUM OF FINE ARTS

BY
IVÁN FENYŐ

OCTOBER HOUSE / NEW YORK

First published in the United States of America 1966 by
October House Inc.
134 East 22nd Street
New York, N.Y. 10010

Library of Congress Catalog Card No. 66-14731
Printed in Hungary

CONTENTS

INTRODUCTION 7

CATALOGUE 25

Addenda and Corrigenda 178

PLATES 179

APPENDIX i

List of Drawings Connected With Paintings and Prints iii

Bibliography v

List of Figures xix

List of Plates xx

Index xxiv

- Names of Artists xxiv
- Names of Places xxviii

The significance of the collection of drawings of the Museum of Fine Arts in Budapest is well known to experts, amateurs and connoisseurs of old drawings alike. However, as a rule, they, too, are acquainted only with the principal items: the unique sheets of Leonardo, Raphael, Correggio, Tintoretto, Veronese, Dürer and Rembrandt. It is astonishing how few of these drawings have been published outside of Hungary. Although some of them were published in Hungarian art periodicals, they have remained practically unknown to international art researchers. Thus the two fine facsimile volumes of Lajos Vayer and Dénes Pataky bring to light, most impressively, genuine treasures which have been virtually unknown hitherto.[1]

The Museum of Fine Arts' collection is by no means of lesser importance than that of the National Picture Gallery which is rightly renowned. Admittedly the collection of drawings is no match for the rich collections in Vienna, Paris or London, to mention only a few. But although it does not contain a single drawing by Michelangelo and only one by Rubens, and whereas the draughtsmanship of Bruegel is represented in it by a dubious sheet only, it nevertheless contains a rich variety of drawings illuminating the development of European graphic art.

With respect to quantity the Italian material is predominant, and within it the group of North Italian sheets is outstanding. Not only does this group exceed the rest of Italian schools numerically but also illustrates more uniformly and with relative clarity and completeness the trend of development. In recent years the author concentrated his research work in this field and investigated the drawings belonging to the North Italian artistic circle. In this way the material revealed from the point of view of art history was quite extensive indeed; the impressive number of high quality drawings induced the author finally to include them in the framework of a book.

'North Italian Art' is understood first and foremost to mean the art of Venice—and of the mainland, the so-called *Terra ferma*, which embraces the City of the Lagoons in a semi-circle, and which is really identical with the Veneto region. However, the artists of Padua, Vicenza, Verona, Brescia and Bergamo belong to the same circle. Piedmont and Lombardy as well as Genoa, Cremona and Parma also come under the North Italian School. The city of Ferrara has been left out from this circle because her art is related rather with Bologna's sphere of activity. For the same reason artists like Niccolò dell'Abbate of Modena have been omitted, though he continued the graphic achievements of Parmigianino. However, the impulses he had received from the Bologna master Primaticcio were of far greater significance in his art; furthermore Parmigianino's effect on him was indirect and was brought to bear upon him through the intermediary of Primaticcio.

[1] Lajos Vayer: Master Drawings. Budapest, 1957.
Dénes Pataky: From Delacroix to Picasso. Budapest, 1959.

This work is not aimed at presenting the whole stock of North Italian drawings of the collection, which will devolve upon a scientific catalogue, to whose preparations the present book, as it were, owes its existence. Here, first of all, the drawings to be dealt with are those that can be brought into connexion with the names of certain artists. Out of the ample stock of the drawings of Parmigianino, Palma il Giovane and Cambiaso, a selection had to be made in accordance with the space available in this volume. In choosing the sheets with regard to artistic quality, the circumstance of their having been previously unknown also had to be taken into consideration. The same holds true for the works of some masters of lesser importance, like Novelli, Sacchetti and Torretti. Some drawings whose attribution problems could not be unequivocally solved so far have also been included. Their attribution may be established by bringing them to the attention of experts engaged in research.

Now a few words about how the collection came into being. Its bulk—as well as the greatest part of the paintings in the Picture Gallery—originates from the Esterházy collection. Regarding the establishment of the Esterházy collection I have relied upon the following data of the late Simon Meller, the former merited head of the Museum's Department of Prints and Drawings, who, having thoroughly investigated the pertinent sources, wrote the history of the collection.[1]

The Esterházy family's fostering of the arts and passion for collecting were old traditions dating back to the beginning of the seventeenth century. It was then that the Palatine Miklós Esterházy, founder of the family fortune and creator of its political importance, established a kind of *Kunst- und Wunderkammer* in his castle at Fraknó. Although this collection could not be compared with the similar *Kunstkammer* Ferdinand I had brought into being in Vienna in 1563, or with the Archduke Ferdinand of Tyrol's collection at his Castle Ambras, or with Rudolph's *Kunstkammer* in Prague, Esterházy took them as his model.

In the eighteenth century Prince Miklós (1714—1790), called 'the Magnificent,' had his hunting-lodge at Süttör transferred into the gorgeous house of Eszterháza—the *Esterházysche Feenreich* as Goethe termed it ("*Dichtung und Wahrheit*," Part One). Here the Prince held his court from 1768 onwards and created a cultural centre where everybody of rank and fame gathered on the occasion of festivals and receptions. In the opera-house which stood in the park the conductor was Joseph Haydn, he "whose genius spread its wings at Eszterháza." The Empress Maria Theresa herself was among the illustrious guests in 1773, and so was Albrecht von Sachsen-Teschen, the founder of the Albertina of Vienna, who from that time on frequently visited the Prince. The gallery already contained several hundreds of paintings, and Miklós Esterházy

[1] Simon Meller: Az Esterházy Képtár története [The History of the Esterházy Gallery]. Budapest, 1915.

was interested in collecting engravings as well. The following passage is from a description of Eszterháza, dated 1784: "There are to be found there [in the library]. . . a number of excellent old and new engravings by the best masters, many maps and diverse drawings."[1]

However, the real founder of the picture gallery and to an even greater extent of the graphic collection was Prince Miklós Esterházy (1765—1833), the grandson of Miklós the Magnificent. In contrast to the subjective character of collecting which prevailed in the eighteenth century, Prince Miklós collected systematically, according to the historic approach of the neo-classicist period. His cultured sense of art prevented him from being prejudiced against certain epochs, though, up to a point, the Rococo may have been an exception to this. For the only eighteenth-century sheet of really outstanding quality originating from the Esterházy collection is the peerlessly beautiful drawing by Francesco Guardi, "*The Campo SS. Giovanni e Paolo*," in the Museum of Fine Arts in Budapest. Of course, it should be taken into consideration that—in harmony with the taste of the period—there were probably fewer drawings of this kind offered to the Prince for sale, since their prices were low in those days. On the other hand, this does not apply to such an extent with regard to the paintings. As evidenced by the paintings of Sebastiano Ricci, Pellegrini, Magnasco and Bellotto in the Picture Gallery, Prince Miklós Esterházy had a taste for Italian works of art of the eighteenth century, too. First of all it should be borne in mind that in 1821 he purchased Giovanni Battista Tiepolo's "The Victory of St. James the Greater over the Saracens," a painting which today is one of the gems of eighteenth-century painting in possession of the Museum.

Only a few items of his ancestors' collection were considered by the Prince as worthy of inclusion in his collection. As early as 1794—1795 he bought a great number of paintings and engravings in Italy, and in the following year he purchased the collection of engravings of the Counts József and Miklós Pálffy. We do not know what this collection contained but presumably, in addition to engravings, it also comprised drawings. We do know, however, that in the following years the Prince bought numerous engravings, and along with them drawings most certainly were added to the collection.[2] In 1801 the Prince bought many drawings belonging to the famous 'Praun Cabinet' of Nuremberg, from the firm of Frauenholz et Cie. Apart from sheets by Altdorfer, Dürer and Wolf Huber the collection also contained superb Italian drawings, among them master-drawings, such as those of Parmigianino, Annibale Carracci and Lelio Orsi. The

[1] Beschreibung des Hochfürstlichen Schlosses Eszterháza im Königreich Ungarn. Preßburg, by Anton Löwe, 1784. The book was published anonymously but Meller assumed that its author had been Pater Niemecz Primitivus. The Pater was a musician and an admirer of Joseph Haydn. In his old age he became the Prince's librarian.

[2] In these years as well as in subsequent ones the Prince bought graphic works from the following art dealers: Mollo et Cie, Franz Xaver Stöckl, Johann Cappi and Artaria et Cie, all of Vienna, moreover Franz and Dominic Artaria of Mannheim.

Praun Collection along with the Imhoff *Kunstkammer*, also of Nuremberg, were the two greatest patrician collections of the German late Renaissance.

However, it was only from 1803 onwards that the systematic development of the graphic collection was carried out. It was then that the Prince, while in Paris, met the notable Viennese painter and graphic artist Joseph Fischer (1769—1822) who at the Vienna Academy had been a pupil of Johann Christian Brand and of Ferdinand Schmutzer, and on whom, as early as 1793, the title of distinction 'Imperial and Royal Engraver' was conferred. In 1803, the year when they first met, Joseph Fischer entered the Prince's service. First he was Inspector of the collection of paintings and engravings and later—from 1811 on—its Director. In the last year but one of his life he was appointed a Professor at the Vienna Academy. In Joseph Fischer the Prince found a collaborator for whom the development of the collection was a matter of intimate concern, and who devoted his expert knowledge, first and foremost, to the purchase of engravings. Certainly, it was partly due to his influence that scarcely a month after his return from Paris, Prince Miklós Esterházy bought the collection of drawings and engravings of the Count Franz Anton Nowohradsky-Kollowrath in Prague. We cannot now form an accurate conception of the size of this collection. However, we know at least a part of it from the series of engravings made by Joseph Schmidt of nineteen drawings in the collection, at the end of the eighteenth century. From these engravings we know that such outstanding master-drawings as Rembrandt's "Peasant Yard" in two variants and the "Woman with Weeping Child and Dog" originate from the Prague collection.[1]

From 1804 on the amounts paid for the purchase of engravings and drawings tended to increase. The most significant addition to Esterházy's collection took place in 1810 when the Prince bought in Paris the splendid collection of the well-known 'marchand-amateur' Antonio Cesare Poggi who was a native of Parma. It included the three sketches of Leonardo—two of heads for "The Battle of Anghiari" and the study of horses' legs (most probably for the Sforza monument); Raphael's drawing of Psyche, three sheets of Correggio (recently discovered), drawings by Fra Bartolommeo, Giorgione, Romanino, Veronese, Parmigianino, Pontormo, Luini, the Carraccis, and by Reni, Castiglione, etc., to name only a few of the Italians; moreover, the works of the northern masters. Drawings by Rembrandt, Poussin, Claude Lorrain, Jordaens and a great many others originate from this exquisite collection bought in Paris.

In the year 1815 the Esterházy Gallery was opened to the public in the former Kaunitz Palace at Mariahilf in Vienna, bought by Prince Miklós Esterházy a short time before. The graphic collection which had been earlier housed in the Palace of the Hungarian Guards was allotted three rooms in the Kaunitz

[1] Recueil d'Estampes d'après les Dessins originaux qui se trouvent à Prague dans la Collection de François Antoine Comte Nowohradsky-Kollowrath gravées par Joseph Schmidt. Premier cahier contenant onze estampes d'après Rembrandt van Ryn et deux d'après Hochstraten.

Palace at that time. Miklós Esterházy continually cared for the collection, and his sister, the Princess Grassalkovich, as well as his favourite daughter Leopoldine, the Princess von Liechtenstein, also took great interest in enriching it. It is noteworthy that Leopoldine Esterházy was herself a talented artist, which is proved by a drawing by her recently published at the Museum of Bassano. The work displays the finest traditions of Venetian landscape painting in the style of Marco Ricci and Zuccarelli.[1]

In 1805 Antonio Canova was a guest at the Prince's Palace at Kismarton. He made various drawings of Leopoldine and also modelled her several times.

It was due to the constant efforts of both the princely family and Joseph Fischer who selected and bought from the astonishing amount of graphic works abounding on the contemporary Vienna market that the Esterházy collection along with the Albertina soon became the most remarkable graphic collection in Vienna.

Prince Miklós Esterházy bequeathed to his son a considerable collection: a picture gallery of 1,156 paintings, and a graphic collection of about 3,500 drawings and 50,000 engravings, the bulk of which had been acquired by him. With his decease the development of the collection came to an end. His heirs only preserved the collection but did not augment it. Towards the middle of the nineteenth century the tension between Vienna and the movement for Hungary's independence was growing higher and higher, and it finally culminated in the Hungarian War of Independence in 1848—1849. In the years of oppression that followed the defeat of the uprising, Prince Pál Esterházy, the then owner of the collection, transferred it to Pest in 1865, presumably in the spirit of solidarity with his native Hungary. Here the collection was housed in rooms furnished for this purpose, in the building of the Hungarian Academy of Sciences, an edifice completed not long before.

Then, however, a decisive turn came. In 1870 Pál Esterházy's son, Miklós Esterházy, sold to the Hungarian State the collection which then consisted of 637 paintings, the graphic collection which comprised 3,535 drawings, 51,301 engravings and 305 volumes.[2] By this transaction the Esterházy collection as such had ceased to exist. As early as in 1871 the National Picture Gallery came into being, and out of it, towards the last years of the century, the Hungarian National Museum of Fine Arts was developed. The present building of the Museum was completed in 1906.

In 1901 there occurred an event of great importance for the history of the collection which by then belonged to the state: Stefan Delhaes, a painter of

[1] Licisco Magagnato: Disegni del Museo Civico di Bassano. Catalogo della Mostra. Venice, 1956, No. 94.

[2] The total amount paid for the collection came up to 1,300,000 Gulden, "which testified to the generosity and patriotism of Prince Esterházy because at the same time a London art dealer had offered over 2,000,000 Gulden for the collection," wrote Simon Meller.

Belgian origin living in Vienna, but who had been born in Hungary and had always professed himself a Hungarian, bequeathed his graphic art collection to the Hungarian State. The bequest consisted of about 14,500 engravings and more than 2,500 drawings. It was of special importance that Austrian and Italian art of the eighteenth century was richly represented in his collection and thus a gap in the collection of the Museum was at least partly filled.

Among the North Italian drawings from the Delhaes bequest special mention should be made of some important sheets, such as those of Parmigianino, Camillo Bocaccino, Giulio Cesare Procaccini, Carpioni, Diziani, Fontebasso and Zais. Nor should the considerable collection of the works of the stage designer Lorenzo Sacchetti be overlooked. (At the time of the Delhaes bequest the creators of most of these drawings had not yet been identified. The same refers, by the way, to the sheets of the Esterházy collection as well.)

After the generous donation of Stefan Delhaes the rate of expansion of the graphic collection of the Museum slowed down. Only a few notable purchases of drawings belonging to the group of North Italian masters took place in later decades; among these were the characteristic sheet of Domenico Tiepolo, the "Assumption of the Virgin," which was acquired for the collection in 1914, a drawing by Bellotto in 1918 and the precious sketch-book with studies of animals, a work of Lombardy, perhaps originating in the first half of the fifteenth century. In 1923 Gustav Nebehay presented to the Museum the first drawing by Giovanni Battista Tiepolo, an animated study of one of the principal figures of the fresco on the staircase in the archbishop's residence at Würzburg. A few years later Simon Meller, who in the meantime had quit his position in the Museum, enriched the collection with two further drawings by Giovanni Battista Tiepolo. The sheet with the head of St. James the Apostle, drawn by Domenico Tiepolo after the above-mentioned painting by Giambattista, was also donated by Simon Meller.

That is about all the notable North Italian drawings that were acquired in the first half of the twentieth century.

Following such outstanding predecessors as Gábor Térey (who had particular ability for sorting out the engravings) and Simon Meller, Edith Hoffmann took charge of the Department of Prints and Drawings of the Museum of Fine Arts in 1921 and ran it for twenty-five years. It is to her scientific approach that we owe the arrangement of the stock of drawings; the preparation of an inventory of the predominant part of the stock and the establishment of a thorough handwritten catalogue. With an admirable knowledge of the material and a splendid memory for forms, she investigated the prints with which the drawings of the Budapest collections could be related. Her writings on this theme are of lasting value and of particular importance with respect to the catalogues now being prepared. During the period between the two world wars Edith Hoffmann published her attributions of drawings in the Year-Books of the Museum of

Fine Arts. By investigating the paintings with which the drawings she dealt with could be connected, she applied exemplary methods that may well serve as models for all art scholars. Here, too, her eminent knowledge of the rich material of the Museum was most helpful; she identified a great number of important prints, among them sheets of Luini, Bernardo Castello, Malosso, Ansaldo, Zanetti and others of the circle of North Italian art. It is due to her, first and foremost, that our magnificent drawing by Paolo Veronese "Peter of Amiens before the Doge" could be firmly established within the master's *oeuvre*. Owing to the firm foundations, on which she based her attributions, the overwhelming majority of the results published in her articles are of lasting validity.

In arranging the material and establishing the handwritten catalogue, Edith Hoffmann set out from the principle of strict scientific criticism. On the other hand it was a feature characteristic not only of her work in these decades (the 1920s and 1930s) that research on art, particularly if confined to drawings, fell into the mistake of being hyper-critical—as though by way of a reaction to the positivist *Kunstanschauung* of the nineteenth century. The opinion prevailed that the requirements of 'scientific objectivity' would be met by judging works of art more strictly than was proper. By this strictness 'emotional and subjective evaluations' were to be banned from the history of art. That is why in collections of drawings even outstanding sheets were relegated to the 'second rank' material *(zweite Garnitur)* or, even more frequently, were regarded as inferior pieces of the collection, as they were considered to be copies. As a matter of fact the very expression 'copy' was deprived of its original and rather unequivocal meaning to stand for a negative evaluation of quality. Of course, this does not mean that today or in the future drawings should be judged less severely than before. However, one does not proceed less scientifically if the result of an investigation in the history of art is not totally a negative one. This manner of valuation makes itself felt over and over again concerning the Budapest collection, especially when the question 'original or copy' is to be decided.

After Edith Hoffmann's death in 1945, first Jolán Balogh and then Lajos Vayer took charge of the Department of Prints and Drawings. In the post-war years they carried out the hard job of reconstruction with the greatest conscientiousness, circumspection and expert knowledge.

It is superfluous to go into details with respect to the development that art literature on drawings has experienced in the past decades. The very field covered by this book offers a telling example of this. In the decades that have elapsed since the Second World War the research on Venetian art has developed particularly well. The blank spots on the map of Venetian graphic art are gradually disappearing, owing to a series of exhibitions of Venetian drawings, scientific catalogues of some significant collections and, last but not least, to the papers published in the excellently edited year-book of the *Arte Veneta*, which has been appearing since 1947.

This development in the research of drawings demands an entirely new analysis of the Budapest stock. Edith Hoffmann established her handwritten catalogue three decades ago. However, it is not only that our knowledge has been extended by new results but the number of drawings has also considerably grown. These sheets—nearly two thousand in number—are not new acquisitions. They belonged to the collection when the Museum was established but they remained absolutely unknown. Among a heap of material that was qualified as worthless, there was a large number of sheets which not only deserved being inventoried but turned out to be important drawings by eminent artists. These discoveries are a most welcome 'interior' enrichment of the collection in that they were acquired without purchases. The greatest sheet of this 'excavated' material may well be a drawing by Rembrandt. But among other important drawings the author could identify the works of a great number of North Italian masters as well, including Parmigianino, Tintoretto, Palma il Giovane, Lelio Orsi, Bassetti, Carlotto, Bazzani, Fontebasso, Zais, etc.

The considerable number of drawings hitherto completely unknown has been increased by the discovery of numerous sheets inventoried as copies which the author recognized as valuable originals of important artists. A further augmentation of the material resulted from the new attribution of several drawings that had already figured in Edith Hoffmann's handwritten catalogue.

All these changes had a marked effect on the whole structure of the estimation and assessment of the collection of Italian drawings in Budapest. For this reason it is particularly important to begin a scientific cataloguing of the drawings. This work is of especial urgency also because—as already mentioned—only a small fraction of the collection has been recorded so far in the literature of art history and the bulk of the stock of drawings has remained *terra incognita* for researchers.

As mentioned before, the present work is not aimed at substituting a catalogue that comprises all the drawings. Only if a drawing raises no problems of whatever nature from the point of view of its classification in art history, is it to be dealt with in the concise terms of a catalogue. Or else, as is the case with the four studies of heads (Figs. 22, 23 and Pls. 90, 91), the drawing is explained in a few sentences only because the author has not succeeded in overcoming the uncertainty regarding its date or its place of origin, let alone solving the riddle of which master created it. But where the analysis exceeds the dimensions of a catalogue (as for example in the case of the sheet of Francesco Bonsignori—Liberale da Verona, or the drawing that had to be denied attribution to Titian), the reader is requested not to consider these analyses as data of a catalogue, but as a short study. With regard to drawings, which the author has already published in earlier works, he has had to content himself with giving summaries of the results.

*

Only few sheets in the Budapest Museum represent North Italian drawings of the fifteenth century. The names of the century's great draughtsmen, of Pisanello, Mantegna, Bellini and Carpaccio, are missing. But early anonymous drawings are also of great significance since they convey a vivid representation of North Italian graphic art of that time.

The drawing—probably from Bologna—made about 1400 and entitled "Hunting Adventure" (Pl. 1) has been long known in art history and has been appreciated as an important example of this early style. Much less known, however, is the fine sketch-book with drawings of animals, a work whose enchanting and graceful artistic idiom refers to Lombardy (Pls. 2, 3). One of the sheets of highest quality in the small group of early North Italian masters is the majestic "Madonna" by Bartolomeo Montagna who was a follower of Giovanni Bellini and a leading master of the Vicenza school (Pl. 10). The soft blue tint of the wash greatly enhances the beauty of the drawing. Closely connected in style with it is a study of a recumbent woman, originating from about 1500 (Pl. 8). It used to be considered Florentine work; however, in addition to its pictorial softness it is first of all due to the way the outlines of the figure are made to emerge by means of internal hatching that its Venetian origin is revealed. The author supposes it to be by Basaiti. "The Construction of the Argo" suggests Andrea Mantegna but it shows only a faint reflection of the master's powerful personality (Pl. 7). The most fascinating feature of this drawing is rather the singular allegoric subject whose iconologic analysis was recently presented in a splendid article by Erwin Panofsky.

Three drawings by Correggio which not long ago were concealed among the copies are regarded today as belonging to the most valuable treasures of the collection (Pls. 16—18). However, a drawing which twenty years ago was brought into connexion with no less a name than that of Giorgione's still remains questionable (Pl. 12). To make a decision in this case is almost impossible since Giorgione's graphic art is still a complete mystery. Apart from the Castelfranco sheet in Rotterdam, every drawing tentatively attributed to him presents a difficult problem. Anyhow, the sheet is of an exceptionally high quality, and all researchers that had the opportunity to see the original drawing agreed with this attribution. Only Antonio Morassi doubted Giorgione's authorship but he did not degrade the drawing either by attributing it to Giovanni Bellini.—The drawing "The Bearing of the Cross" was considered by Detlev von Hadeln as a Titian (Pl. 21); but a strict criticism of the style does not permit this distinguished attribution. The loss of this 'Titian' may be somewhat compensated for by a brilliant and hitherto unknown drawing of a Bishop, which reflects Titian's spirit much more than the sheet mentioned above (Pl. 26). This is a highly instructive example of the early style of the Cremona artist Camillo Boccaccino in the period when he was completely spellbound by Titian. Among North Italian drawings the one representing "A Hilly Landscape" is a very interesting curiosity and *unicum.*

According to the attributions of A. M. Hind, Edith Hoffmann and Otto Benesch it is presumably a work of Domenico Campagnola's, which a century later—when the drawing belonged to him—was 'corrected' by Rembrandt according to his own taste and that of his own period (Pl. 25).

The drawing which represents two fashionably dressed ladies holding hands and dancing to the lute accompaniment of their two escorts is imbued with a particular charm (Pl. 27). The author exhibited this sheet in 1960 under the fairly general attribution '*Anonimo Giorgionesco*,' having picked it out from among a mass of unrecognized drawings. Giuseppe Fiocco, the' Great Old Man' of Venetian art historical research, thought of Marcello Fogolino in connexion with this sheet, and in the following year Lionello Puppi published it as Fogolino's work. Fogolino's art had sprung from that of Vicenza, the circle of Bartolomeo Montagna. Later on he worked in a style that was related to that of Giorgione's followers (i.e. of the young Titian, Giulio and Domenico Campagnola, and then Romanino). The author does not think the attribution to Fogolino fully convincing, however much the romantic and graceful style of the drawing seems to reflect the effect of Giorgione's elegic style upon Fogolino.

The wide range of Parmigianino's drawings, out of which seven sheets are published here (Pls. 28—34), is a particularly precious group among North Italian drawings. The upswing of the research of Italian drawings has resulted, in different collections, in an increase of the graphic *oeuvre* of Parmigianino, the great draughtsman of the city of Parma. (E.g. in the Albertina.) In Budapest, too, the new investigations led to the identification of a great number of his works, whereas only one or two dubious sheets had to be deducted from his *oeuvre*. A. E. Popham, the eminent scholar and expert on Parmigianino's graphic art, published in the "Bulletin of the Museum of Fine Arts" numerous sheets misjudged before. The author has continued his investigation and has identified a great number of other drawings. Detailed reports on the results of these investigations were partly published in "*Arte Antica e Moderna*" and partly in "The Burlington Magazine." Thus whereas five or six years ago there were altogether only about four sheets by Parmigianino in the Budapest collection, today twenty-four of his drawings are preserved there.

A particularly interesting and beautiful Parmigianino drawing in Budapest shows on the *recto* St. Cecilia and on the *verso* sketches of David (Pls. 28, 29). The importance of this drawing lies not only in its truly Raphaelesque beauty. To the art historian it is of such particular significance because it is a hitherto unknown study for one of Parmigianino's paintings, namely "St. Cecilia" on the organ shutter in the church Sta. Maria della Steccata, Parma. As there is a close connexion in style between the sheet and the frescoes of Fontanellato, it throws a new light upon their date of origin, too. This offers a further argument that these frescoes, illuminated with Raphaelesque beauty, are to be considered as Parmigianino's early works and not late ones as presumed before.

The rest of his drawings published here are doubtlessly late works of the master who passed away in his prime. The date of the sheet "A Woman Seated at a Table" is offered by its *verso* on which there are figures of girls, made as sketches for the Steccata frescoes (Pls. 30, 31). The decorative sheet entitled "Proserpina Changing Ascalaphus into an Owl" (Pl. 32) originates from the same time, whereas the drawing "Venus with Cupid" (Pl. 34) leads us to the last period of Parmigianino's as a draughtsman, and the peculiar representation of the two seated female nudes may be put at an even later date (Pl. 33). In this last period the artist in his elongated nudes dispensed with the aesthetic beauty of lines which had been given so eminent a role and meaning in the earlier phases, nor did he insist upon anatomic correctness of the drawing. In these very latest pen-drawings he also omitted the wash he was wont to add with a brush. The stress is laid upon the internal contents of the representation. It might be some scene connected with the experiments of Parmigianino's last years.

First and foremost it was Correggio and Michelangelo who exerted an effect on Lelio Orsi. He condensed these influences in his strangely dream-like creations. The author has been able to identify two interesting and characteristic drawings by his hand (Pls. 37—39). The peculiar sheet entitled "The Creation of the World" —whose fantastic features suggest a William Blake of the sixteenth century— inspired a highly interesting iconological analysis by Erwin Panofsky.

Sixty-five drawings in the Museum are connected with the art of the Genoese artist Luca Cambiaso. His manneristic and characteristic style of drawing was most popular in the second half of the sixteenth and in the beginning of the seventeenth centuries. Many artists copied him, and even higher was the number of his imitators; thus it is by no means an easy job to pick out the originals from among the host of so-called Cambiaso drawings. The bulk of the drawings in the Budapest collection turned out to be copies. There are, however, four sheets published here whose authenticity can hardly be doubted (Pls. 40—43). Particular interest must be accorded to "The Last Judgement" if only for the circumstance that it is incontestably his own work which nevertheless differs from his other drawings which display over and over the artistic idiom of his mannerism. Johannes Wilde's keen eyes recognized in the sheet the master's handwriting.

Our Tintoretto drawings—studies after the so-called Atlas—are well known in art literature. And yet, it should be duly pointed out that they are among the master's most beautiful drawings (Pls. 46—49). The black and white reproduction, of course, gives little idea of the beauty of the original which with black and white chalk on the blue Venetian paper conveys a most impressive effect.

Very well known, too, in the Budapest collection is Veronese's drawing "Peter of Amiens before the Doge Vitale Michiel" (Pls. 54, 55). Hardly any other drawing of similar beauty is known by this master's hand. The sheet with the monumental design of a tomb, which—according to Giorgio Vasari—represents a joint work of Paolo Veronese and Andrea Palladio, originates from Vasari's collection, one of the earliest collections of drawings (Pl. 53). For the second edition of his "*Vite*" Vasari set up a series of five volumes of plates and himself drew the cartouche-frames for the sheets. One of these sheets is published here. According to the style and quality of the drawing, we have no reason for doubting the truth of Vasari's inscription to be found on the sheet:

ANDREA PALLADIO
ARCHITETTOR. VICE.
le figure son di Paolo Veronese.

Below these words the following inscription, written in a different dark ink, can be read: "*fuit Georgii Vasari, nunc P. J. Mariette 1741.*" Two more sheets, also attributed to Veronese, are of very high artistic value, too. "Christ in the House of Simon" is not unknown to the literature of art; already Meder published it in his work "*Die Handzeichnung*" (Pl. 57). It reflects so convincingly the festive and joyful atmosphere of Veronese's art, moreover it contains so many details similar to those in his other drawings that there can be scarcely any doubt about its authenticity. On the other hand, up to now "The Execution of a Martyr," considered by Philip Pouncey as Veronese's work, was absolutely unknown (Pl. 56). According to traditions it also ranks as a Veronese, though here it is not the artist of gorgeous and sensuous festivities who speaks to us, but the master of dramatic power and passion, in the same vein as in the painting "Crucifixion" in the Budapest Museum of Fine Arts.

With respect to Palma il Giovane, this untiring draughtsman of late Venetian mannerism, the Budapest collection gives rise to the same statements as are made about Parmigianino. Only a few years ago there was not a single drawing in Budapest that could have been attributed to him with certainty but today a number of sheets characteristic of him can be published (Pls. 59—66). There are such important drawings among them as "The Miracle of the Loaves" purchased a few years ago (Plate 65a), which is a preliminary sketch to the painting of the same title in the church Maria del Carmine in Venice; or the red chalk drawing "St. Jerome," whose softness nearly suggests Guercino's drawings (Pl. 63). The author discovered drawings in the Budapest Museum of such North Italian territories as had been unknown before. Mention should be made here of two sheets by the Piedmont mannerist Guglielmo Caccia detto il Moncalvo (Pls. 70, 71). One of these can be related to an altarpiece at Piacenza (Pl. 71 and Fig. 17). We have published another sheet with a putto in the Bulletin No. 22 of the Museum in 1963.

The new results comprise some characteristic and fine examples of late mannerist or early Baroque artists of Lombardy. These artists continued the traditions of the highly passionate style of Gaudenzio Ferrari's drawings. One of these sheets, by Giulio Cesare Procaccini (again an excellent attribution by Philip Pouncey), is among the artist's finest drawings and also points to the Venetian elements in his art, which—as far as the author knows—had not been emphasized before (Pls. 74, 75). Two drawings of Morazzone's, very characteristic of this artist, are being published here for the first time. By means of an old engraving Mina Gregori (authoress of the thorough and scientifically founded catalogue of the Morazzone exhibition held in Varese in 1962) ascertained that one of the Budapest drawings had served as a sketch for the series of frescoes, which in the meantime had been destroyed, of the church Sant'Angelo in Milan (Pl. 77). Most probably the other drawing in Budapest had also been made for the same series of frescoes (Pl. 76 and Fig. 16). This small Lombardic group is completed by two sheets of Giovanni Mauro della Rovere, who was a pupil of Camillo Procaccini but was also strongly influenced by Morazzone (Pls. 78, 79). The same expressionistic tendencies prevail in Rovere's art as are characteristic of Giulio Cesare Procaccini and even more of Morazzone.

The Seicento exhibition staged in Venice in 1959 made it clear what a number of unsolved attribution problems the graphic art of Venice in the seventeenth century still offers to research. One of the reasons why this is so may well be the astonishingly small number of drawings from Venice or from the Veneto of that period. The more gratifying is the reappearence of drawings in the Budapest collection in these past years which have proved to be works of notable Venetian artists. Side by side with the peculiar and characteristic drawing of the Verona artist Marcantonio Bassetti (Pl. 80), the hitherto absolutely unknown sheet of Johann Carl Loth, a native of Munich, is also to be included among the Seicento drawings of Venice (Pl. 85). The sheet is a preparatory sketch for one of his best-known paintings. However, it also plays an important part in the artist's graphic *oeuvre* which has not been sufficiently clarified up to now. In the same way the author has been able to attribute a drawing to Pietro Liberi (Pl. 89). This one, too, is a preparatory sketch to a painting of the artist's, which was published a few years ago by N. Ivanoff. Nor was Carpioni represented in the collection in the past. The two drawings in red chalk are not only highly characteristic of his art but belong to his most beautiful sheets (Pls. 86, 87). No superficiality or clumsiness of the lines—which otherwise rather often occur in Carpione's sketches—are to be observed in them. Only with some reservations can a sheet be attributed to Domenico Fetti and another one to Sebastiano Mazzoni (Pls. 81, 82), although it seems likely that these attributions will be endorsed by experts.

The opinion about the two Strozzi drawings of the collection is not unanimous (Pls. 83, 84). The inscription "Lodovico Carracci" to be found on the sheet "Christ and the Woman of Samaria" gave Otto Benesch some food for thought. Lodovico Carracci might have been the maker of the drawing. (Oral information.) Regarding the other sheet, "Christ in the House of Simon," Strozzi's name has become traditional, and Edith Hoffmann convincingly proved its connexion with Strozzi's *oeuvre.* In both cases the author accepts Strozzi, this great Genoese-Venetian artist, to have been the draughtsman of the two sheets. Some other fine sheets represent Genoese graphic art in the collection. First to be mentioned are the colourful and exquisite drawings of G. B. Castiglione, the interesting "Medici Allegory" by Ansaldo and the delicately tinted "Madonna" by Biscaino (Pls. 92—97).

Thus we have reached the Settecento. Eighteenth-century North Italian drawings are abundantly represented in the collection but unfortunately this richness does not refer to the very greatest artists of the epoch. It is a most regrettable gap that there is no drawing in the collection by Giovanni Battista Piazzetta who was equally phenomenal both as a draughtsman and as a printer. Antonio Canale is also missing. A sketch masterly in its sweep and its lightness of touch, "Hercules on the Cross-Roads," has been attributed by the author to Sebastiano Ricci, the pioneering artist of the Rococo (Pl. 99). The Prints and Drawings Department of the Museum acquired this sheet in 1958. With it we have reached the deceitful ground of the problems concerning the drawings of Sebastiano Ricci, Giovanni Antonio Pellegrini, Gaspare Diziani and Francesco Fontebasso. These problems, particularly in connexion with the great number of sheets by Gaspare Diziani, will be looked into in greater detail in the part of the present volume containing the catalogue.

The three sheets by Giambattista Tiepolo have already been mentioned as acquisitions of the Museum (Pls. 118—121). The sketch for the fresco of the Archbishop's residence in Würzburg displays on its *verso* the head of a woman (perhaps of a Madonna), which has not been published yet. Julius von Schlosser commented as follows on this most majestic type of Tiepolo's female figures: "... *Sein Frauentypus überhaupt berührt uns oft seltsam widerspruchsvoll mit seinem etwas sinnlichen und doch fast hochmütig abweisenden Ausdruck, in dem eine feine Mischung von Koketterie und Kälte liegt.*" With rare understanding Schlosser in this fine study made a plea for Tiepolo and his period as early as 1898, although the art of the eighteenth century was not held in too high esteem at the turn of the last century.

Francesco Guardi's drawing "*The Campo SS. Giovanni e Paolo in Venice*" with its glimmering strokes of the pen is one of the most beautiful sheets of the collection; and moreover, is, in view of its large dimensions, an important work of the artist's (Pl. 131).

The orbit of the art of S. Ricci, G. B. Tiepolo and F. Guardi is surrounded with a rich variety of 'stars of second order,' although many a drawing of theirs gives the lie to this modest denomination. The author has been able to ascertain that three interesting drawings are the work of Giambattista Pittoni (Pls. 102—104). Although, compared with the Correr drawings of the artist's as well as with his sheets in the Louvre, they appear to be somewhat rigid, the possibility arises that they are copies—but copies made by Pittoni himself. This repetition of his own compositions, by the way, tallies with his working methods because he would transfer certain figures, even certain complete parts, from one work into the other. The three drawings are closely connected with numerous paintings by Pittoni. A most instructive example of what a copy of a Pittoni drawing, made by somebody else's hand, looks like is offered by a fine drawing in the Budapest Museum, made by Pittoni's pupil, the German painter Anton Kern (b. in Tetschen in 1710 and d. in Dresden in 1747) after Pittoni's painting "The Generosity of Scipio" (Fig. 27).[1]

There are sixteen drawings by Gaspare Diziani among the plates illustrating this volume (Pls. 105—117 and Figs. 29, 31).

In the past years a great number of Gaspare Diziani's drawings have been published, and thus the outlines of his graphic style are clearly discernible. His drawings are more significant than his paintings. While as a painter he strikes us as only an imitator of Sebastiano Ricci, his drawings and his careless sketches in oil testify to a powerful personality and a passionate temperament. However, there are phases of style in his development as a draughtsman, which continue to present great problems to the researcher. His early works are strongly blended with the style of his ideals, as seen in the sheets by Sebastiano Ricci and Giovanni Antonio Pellegrini. But a great number of drawings are known from his intermediate period, which in their very peculiarity cannot be mistaken for those of other artists. Most of the Budapest sheets belong to this period of his activity (Pls. 106—111), while the sheet "Boreas, the God of Winds, Abducting Oreithyia" (Pl. 112), but even more "The Rape of Helen" (Pl. 113) are to be set at a later date when his style became intermixed with that of Francesco Fontebasso, twenty years his junior; and at the same time these sheets betray a certain return to Pellegrinesque graphic elements. Regarding these late drawings the handiwork of Diziani could not be completely distinguished from that of Fontebasso. In the clarification of the questions connected with Diziani's art the relevant material, comprising nearly two hundred drawings, is to be found at the Kunstinstitut Städel in Frankfurt. The author perused them in 1962. Notwithstanding a number of common features, the drawings in Frankfurt display differences in style and quality, which can only be explained by the fact that they were made by different artists. At intervals small fraction of the material has already been published, and has been partly attributed to Pellegrini and partly to Diziani.

[1] 394 by 245 mm. (15$^5/_8$''×9$^3/_4$''). Red chalk. From the Esterházy collection. Inv. No. 697. At the bottom an inscription in an old hand, perhaps the artist's own: "Ant Kern delin: aus einem Bilde seines Meisters. Das war seine arth zu zeichnen, welches man grauiren nennet." Pittoni's Scipio painting, along with another of his pictures, "Achilles among Lykomedes' Daughters," the counterpart of the former, was sold at auction under Sebastiano Ricci's name, at the sale of the Wedewer collection at Lepke in Berlin in 1913.

Until not long ago Domenico Tiepolo was represented in the collection by a single sheet (Pl. 123). However, in his excellent work on D. Tiepolo's drawings, which was published in 1962, J. Byam Shaw attributed to him the magnificent head of St. James as well. This brilliant copy by Domenico, after G. B. Tiepolo's famous painting in Budapest "St. James of Compostella on Horseback," had hitherto been considered as a sketch drawn by the painter himself (Pl. 122).

An interesting addition to the eighteenth-century Italian material was provided by a drawing of Giuseppe Bazzani's, "The Presentation at the Temple," with studies of four heads on the *verso* (Pls. 126, 127), which the author published in 1958. Hardly any drawings of the outstanding master of Mantua are known, and none of the sheets attributed to him so clearly displays the style prevailing in his *oeuvre* as a painter. In every single line, in every movement the sheet irradiates the spirit, so individual and so particular, of Bazzani's art. The pathos of the movements also bears witness to his hand. Under the burden of their emotions and passions, the figures bend and bow like trees in a storm. His art is an offspring not only of Italy, his figures and types are, at the same time, the descendants of Peter Paul Rubens. In view of the fact that Bazzani's drawings are rather rare, we are publishing among the figures a drawing, by no means less authentic, which was offered for sale by Budapest art dealers after the Second World War (Fig. 32). We do not know where the sheet is hidden at present, only a good photograph of it is available in the archives of the Museum.

A drawing with figures, most brilliant and witty, by Giovanni Battista Piranesi represents an important addition to the collection (Pl. 135). Mention should also be made of the drawings of Conte Antonio Maria Zanetti, this great collector of Parmigianino drawings, who was a highly cultured dilettante-artist in the best meaning of the word (Pls. 134a and b). They are most instructive examples of the revival of Parmigianino's art in the eighteenth century. The two Madonna drawings were probably made after Parmigianino's sketches to his famous painting in Dresden, the "*Madonna della Rosa*," and were at the same time preparatory sketches to Zanetti's *chiaroscuro* woodcuts which had then again become fashionable and were made after the works of sixteenth-century masters. Two new attributions of landscape drawings should also be pointed out, one by Marco Ricci (Pl. 128) and the other by Giuseppe Zais, which reflects Guardi's influence (Pl. 130). When the present volume had been put to press it was ascertained that a drawing representing a cavalry battle was also Zais' work. Traditionally the sheet had been attributed to Le Bourguignon and it was published under the latter artist's name in Lajos Vayer's volume of facsimiles (No. 89). In 1956 Terisio Pignatti published in *Arte Veneta* drawings by Zais from the Museo Correr, and these works show a striking similarity to the sheet. But at that time the sheet could only be included among the text illustrations (No. 34). The catalogue data are the following: 252 × 408 mm. (10″ × 16¼″). Pen, wash. From the Delhaes collection. Inventory No. 2845. In the left hand bottom an inscription in the same hand as in the above mentioned landscape by Zais with the words "Zucali f.," is almost completely rubbed out, but still clearly legible by quartzlight. Of course, Pietro Antonio Novelli, whose sheets of playful grace show the influence—and often imitation—of Piazzetta, cannot make up for the lack of a Piazzetta (Pls. 136—138). The delicate drawings of stage sets by Fabrizio Galliari again leed us to Piedmont (Pls. 140, 141). A great number of drawings preserved in the collection of the Budapest Museum are by Lorenzo Sacchetti, the famous artist of stage scenery and theatrical design. From among them only a selection can be presented in this volume (Pls. 142—144). With the Rococo artist's zest in playfulness he created, on a sheet of a sketchbook, the illusion of a maquette for stage *décors*, by cutting out the forms with scissors (Pl. 143).

These stage drawings, particularly the early ones, display the same playful lightness as the *vedute* of a Francesco Guardi. Following the line of his scenographic sheets, the course, in which his art developed from late Rococo into the more rigid and geometrical style of Neo-Classicism, can be observed.

This volume contains the results of a work continued for several years. Out of the 144 drawings published here not more than 25 were known to art literature. By publishing it I hope to render some modest service to the research of drawings.

I am deeply obliged to all friends and colleagues who helped me with their observations and advice, and often by encouragement or by sending photographs. Particular thanks are due to Otto Benesch, Alessandro Bettagno, J. Byam Shaw, Bernice Davidson, Bernhard Degenhart, Giuseppe Fiocco, Ernst Gombrich, Nicola Ivanoff, Eckhart Knab, Florence Kossoff, Otto Kurz, Victor Lasareff, Konrad Oberhuber, Rodolfo Pallucchini, Erwin Panofsky, Andor Pigler, Terisio Pignatti, A. E. Popham, Philip Pouncey, Lionello Puppi, Augusta Ghidiglia Quintavalle, János Scholz, Kurt Schwarzweller, Charles de Tolnay and Johannes Wilde.

CATALOGUE

ANONYMOUS, LOMBARDY OR BOLOGNA, BEGINNING OF THE FIFTEENTH CENTURY

HUNTING ADVENTURE

PLATE 1

148×182 mm. (5 7/8″×7 1/4″). Pen and brush in a brownish-grey tone, heightened with body-white on green prepared paper. From the Esterházy collection. Inv. No. 1778.

Literature

Schönbrunner—Meder, Albertina Publication, No. 751; W. Suida, Studien zur lombardischen Malerei. *Monatshefte für Kunstwissenschaft*, 1909, p. 472; P. Toesca, *La pittura e la miniatura nella Lombardia.* Milan, 1912, pp. 452 and 456; R. van Marle, *The Development of the Italian Schools of Painting*, Vol. VII. The Hague, 1926, p. 126 and note; *E. Hoffmann, Magyar Művészet, 1930*, Fig. on p. 181; A. van Schendel, *Le dessin en Lombardie.* Brussels, 1938, p. 55, Plate 28, and p. 126, notes 75—76; B. Degenhart, *Italienische Zeichnungen des frühen 15. Jahrhunderts.* Basel, 1949; L. Vayer, *Master Drawings.* Budapest, 1957, No. 6; *Velencei ... rajzok, 1960*, Cat. No. 129.

The literature dealing with this drawing is very rich indeed. Schönbrunner—Meder reproduced it first under the title of the "Hunting Adventure" and attributed it to an unknown master (after 1400) of Northern Italy. In Wilhelm Suida's opinion it is the work of a master of Lombardy from the beginning of the fifteenth century. He thinks it represents a hunting adventure of the Prince Gian Galeazzo Visconti and is perhaps connected with murals in the latter's palace at Pavia, which depict similar hunting and animal scenes. Pietro Toesca, too, considers it to be the work of a master of Lombardy from the end of the fourteenth or the very beginning of the fifteenth century. The scene makes him think of illustrations to a novel but he does not consider the assertion of similarity with the murals of Pavia convincing. R. van Marle does not think the sheet typical of Lombardic work and also doubts whether the person represented is the Prince Gian Galeazzo Visconti. Arthur van Schendel has no doubt that our drawing is Lombardic and from the end of the fourteenth century. Both in style and in period he relates it to the two most beautiful manuscripts of Lombardic romances in the Bibliothèque Nationale in Paris: "*Lancelot du Lac*" (fr. 343) and "*Guiron le Courtois*" (fr. Nouv. Acq. 5243). Bernhard Degenhart considers this Budapest Museum drawing the work of a master of Bologna and relates it to the chief master of the murals of the Bolognini Chapel of S. Petronio in Bologna, painted at the beginning of the fifteenth century.

In the winter of 1963 the author had the opportunity to see these frescoes, which fully convinced him of Degenhart's attribution being correct. Thus it has happened that it is a Bolognese work that opens the sequence of North Italian drawings. However, only after having put the manuscript to press did the author reconsider the attribution to a Lombardic master.

Anonymous, Lombardy, about 1440

PLATES 2—3 THE PAGES OF A SKETCH-BOOK WITH ANIMAL FIGURES

147×190 mm. ($5^7/_8$″×$7^1/_2$″). Pen and brush drawings on vellum. The sketch-book which comprises 32 pages is in a rather poor condition: decayed and damaged. In most places the drawings have been severely impaired. Presented by dr. Gyula Bischitz. Inv. No. 1918-482.

Literature
E. Hoffmann, *Újszerzeményi kiállítás* [Exhibition of New Acquisitions]. Budapest, 1922, No. 1; L. Vayer, *Master Drawings*. Budapest, 1957, No. 8; *Velencei... rajzok, 1960*, Cat. No. 130.

The sketch-book contains drawings of animals; however, the style and quality of the drawings are not uniform. The same animal is delineated in several variations. Certain sketches of animals are made in a conspicuously heraldic, 'archaistic' style. On the other hand the natural way in which the movements of the animals are depicted on some sheets indicates a direct observation of nature. In these drawings the artist shows a predilection for placing plants and a small part of the ground beside the animals. The draughtsman did not have to travel to the Orient in order to know exotic species of animals, but was able to study them in the zoological gardens that existed in Italy as early as the fourteenth century, e.g. in the Palace of the Viscontis in Pavia. Reference should be made here to the interesting analysis of Otto Pächt (Early Italian Nature Studies. *Journal of the Warburg and Courtauld Institutes*, Vol. XIII, 1950), in which he points out that the illuminators could also copy oriental manuscripts, such as Arabic or Persian bestiaries. Some drawings in the Budapest sketch-book were possibly made after such oriental models. The Budapest book of designs is related to sheets at Bergamo, Venice, London, New York, etc., which partly originate from Giovannino de' Grassi and his workshop. And yet, in spite of this relationship and notwithstanding the fact that we consider it to be Lombardic, strictly speaking, the booklet does not belong to this group. Moreover, in view of the degree of their realism and the motifs of movement, we consider them to have been made some decades later than even the latest drawings belonging to the circle of Giovannino de' Grassi. The sources which first mention this early and important master are dated 1389. Pietro Toesca—whose merit is the reconstruction of Giovannino's art—refers to a connexion of his style with that of Franco-Flemish and of Bohemian miniaturists.

FRANCESCO BONSIGNORI (?)
School of Verona

Born about 1460 in Verona, died 1519 in Coldiero (by Verona). He was influenced by Giovanni Bellini, Alvise Vivarini and Liberale da Verona, but first of all by Andrea Mantegna. In his young years he may have been a pupil of Mantegna's in Mantua, but it is also possible that Mantegna's triptych at San Zeno had an effect on him. In the 'eighties he was staying in Venice and there, apparently, he came under the influence of Antonello da Messina as well. About 1488 he entered the service of the Gonzagas in Mantua. In his late works he expressed himself markedly in the artistic idiom of the Quattrocento. Apart from a few altarpieces, some masterly portraits by him have come down to us. As a draughtsman he is known only through his grandiose, most carefully executed portraits.

THE MADONNA AND CHILD WITH ANGELS PLAYING MUSIC. BENEATH TWO SAINTS: ST. JEROME AND PRESUMABLY ST. AUGUSTINE — PLATE 4
Verso: A SIMILAR REPRESENTATION OF THE MADONNA — FIG. 1

196×129 mm. (7¾″×5⅛″). Pen. From the Esterházy collection. Inv. No. 1768. Pendant of the following drawing (Inv. No. 1767. Plate 5).

Literature
E. Hoffmann, 1931, pp. 132—139, Figs. 4—11; *Velencei ... rajzok, 1960*, Nos. 4 and 6, Fig. 2; *L. Puppi, Arte Veneta, 1959—1960*, Fig. 353; U. B. Schmitt, Francesco Bonsignori. *Münchner Jahrbuch der Bildenden Kunst.* Dritte Folge, Vol. XII, 1961. Sonderdruck. Pp. 73—152, 83, 112—113, Figs. 55—58 and Footnote 125a.

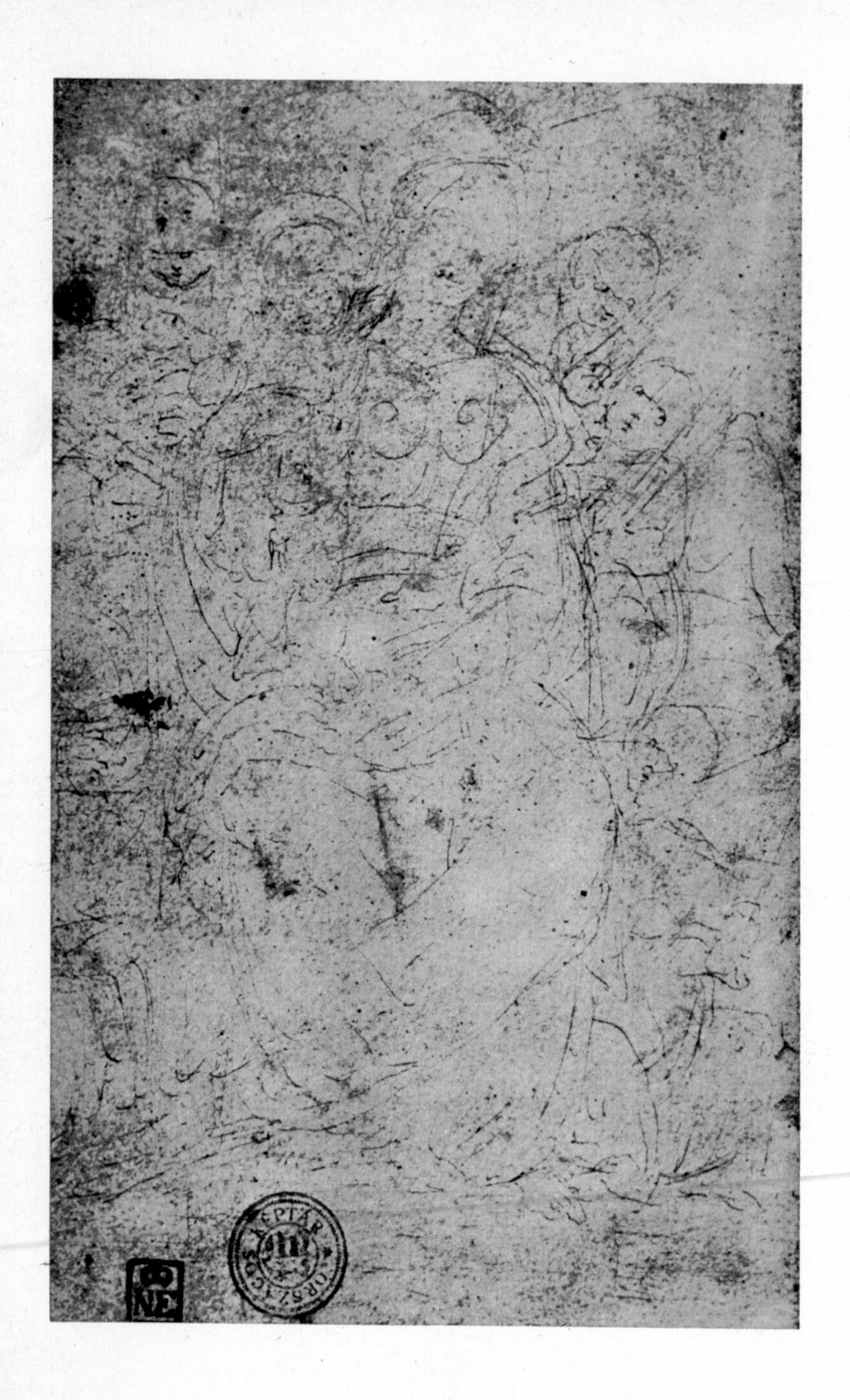

1 Francesco Bonsignori (?):
The Madonna and Child with Angels Playing Music. Verso of Plate 4

This drawing as well as its counterpart had been indicated in the Esterházy collection as Baroccio's (!) works. In the "Year-Book of the Museum of Fine Arts" Edith Hoffmann published it as Francesco Bonsignori's drawing and proved that there were strong links connecting the sheets with the latter master's art. First of all she referred to the altarpiece, dated 1484, of the church S. Fermo Maggiore, which painting, towards the end of the nineteenth century, found its way to the Museo Civico in Verona (Fig. 3). The painting represents the Madonna with the saints Onophrius, Jerome, Augustine and Christopher. On the lower part of the picture there is a portrait in profile of Altabella Avorago dal Bovo who commissioned the painting. Edith Hoffmann based her attribution on the strong conformity of St. Christopher on the *verso* of the drawing of Plate 5 with the same saint in the altarpiece of S. Fermo Maggiore (Fig. 2). The outlines of St. Christopher were retouched by a rough hand at a later date but here and there the original contours in all their exquisite subtlety can still be distinguished. The supposition that the drawing is a copy of the Christopher in the Museo Civico of Verona is contradicted by the slighter and bigger differences noticeable between the two representations, differences which a copyist would not have applied. Edith Hoffmann also pointed to the great resemblance of the figures of St. Jerome and St. Augustine in the drawing of Plate 4 to the same saints in the altarpiece of S. Fermo. In her opinion the hardly discernible Madonna on the *verso* of the drawing shows an unmistakable connexion with the altar Bonsignori painted in the Church of S. Bernardino in 1488, whose composition with the Madonna she quite correctly traced back to Mantegna's altarpiece in S. Zeno. Persuaded by these arguments, we accepted the attribution of the drawings and exhibited them at the 1960 exhibition of the Museum as Bonsignori's works and as unique single examples of his figural compositions as a draughtsman. When reviewing the exhibition in "*Arte Veneta*," Lionello Puppi rejected the attribution. He considered the similarity of the two figures to signify rather a general iconographic conformity than a concrete analogy of style. In an article on Bonsignori, Ursula Barbara Schmitt analysed the two Budapest drawings and attributed them to Liberale da Verona. In her attribution of the two sheets—both of which have drawings on the *recto* as well as on the *verso*—her starting-point was the Madonna on Plate 5, which she believes is a study of Liberale's Madonna in the National Gallery in London (No. 1134). (Fig. 4.) As an explanation for the conformity of the two representations of St. Christopher, Ursula Barbara Schmitt pointed out that Liberale and Bonsignori had a common prototype—possibly Mantegna. In fact the Budapest drawing shows a very close relationship to the London painting. The two Madonnas are as closely related to each other as are the two above-mentioned representations of St. Christopher. But whether the Madonna drawing is indeed a preparatory sketch to the painting in London, cannot be decided. In our opinion no such inference about the artist's person can be drawn, unless an even more concrete explanation can be given, clarifying

2 Francesco Bonsignori (?): St. Christopher. Verso of Plate 5

3 Francesco Bonsignori: Madonna with Saints. Altarpiece from S. Fermo Maggiore. Verona, Museo di Castelvecchio

the connexion between the St. Christopher of the S. Fermo altarpiece and that of the Budapest drawing. When deciding about the authorship, the marked contrast between the Budapest drawings reminiscent in their quiet poise of Antonello da Messina und Giovanni Bellini, and the dynamic, late-Gothic-Baroque art of Liberale da Verona cannot be left out of consideration. No trace of influence from Siena, Florence or Romagna is to be noticed here; that is, influences which make themselves felt in Liberale's art. We have not been able to find that 'exciting and nervous handwriting' in the drawings which reminded U. B. Schmitt of Liberale's miniatures. An example, taken at random and yet most characteristic, is the figure of St. Christopher in Liberale's painting of 1489 which is in Berlin. In its agitation this figure is diametrically opposed to Bonsignori's severe and static St. Christopher and to the saint in the Budapest drawing. Schmitt also finds a close connexion between the Budapest sheet and the one with music-making angels attributed to Liberale and preserved in the British Museum (No. 1895-9-15-590). We cannot perceive such a connexion, the more so as when examining the original drawings the differences strike the eye even more than

in Padua and now in the Museo Civico of the same town) which represents an archer, sitting on the ground and tying up his sandals. In studying the archer's figure, Adolfo Venturi thought he detected the hand of Mantegna (Lucio Grossato. *Il Museo Civico di Padova.* Venice, 1957, pp. 128—129, Plate 63). In Lionello Puppi's opinion it is the work of a less significant artist of the Carpaccio—Bastiani circle. Recently he has attributed these fragments, with a question mark, to Angelo Zotto (L. Puppi, Angelo Zotto et quelques fresques padouanes du XVe siècle. *Bulletin du Musée National Hongrois des Beaux-Arts*, No. 21. Budapest, 1962, pp. 31—43, Plates 20—21).

Lately we discovered a sheet—pen drawing coloured with some gold like the Budapest sheet—similarly with drawings on both sides, attributed to Carpaccio's school, at the Museum Boymans-van Beuningen in Rotterdam (No. I, 491). (Figs. 6, 7.)

To such an extent does the sheet resemble the Budapest one that one not only must attribute both to the same artist, but must also consider the possibility that originally both sheets belonged to the same sketch-book. Let us compare e.g. the group of women in our sheet (Plate 6) with the *recto* of the drawing in Rotterdam (Fig. 6); or the warrior in armour on the bottom right-hand side on the *verso* of our drawing (Fig. 5) with the figure on the right-hand side of the *verso* of the Boymans sheet (Fig. 7). Not only the forms of the body and the postures are identical but the profile of the heads, too, is drawn in the same way: the nose with a strongly emphasized horizontal line at the end, the mouth drawn too long, and the short, dot-like shaping of the part between the mouth and the hooked chin.

Follower of Mantegna, about 1500

PLATE 7 THE CONSTRUCTION OF THE ARGO

358×242 mm. (14⅛"×9½"). Pen with reddish-brown wash. Background blue body-colour, on yellowed paper. From the Esterházy collection. Inv. No. 1770.

Literature

E. Hoffmann, 1930, Cat. No. 24; *Velencei ... rajzok, 1960*, Cat. No. 10; E. Panofsky, La construction de l'Argo en tant qu'allégorie platonicienne. L'iconographie d'un dessin mantegnesque vers 1500. *Bulletin du Musée National Hongrois des Beaux-Arts*, No. 20. Budapest, 1962, pp. 29—33.

In 1960 this drawing was exhibited as the work of a North Italian artist (perhaps of Padua) of about 1500. We remarked in this connexion that it was

5 Anonymous, Venice, end of the fifteenth century: Sheet with astrological (?) symbols. Verso of Plate 6

6 ANONYMOUS, VENICE, END OF THE FIFTEENTH CENTURY: A sheet of sketches. Rotterdam, Museum Boymans-van Beuningen

7 Verso of Fig. 6

9 Marco Basaiti: Detail from "Christ on the Mount of Olives." Venice, Accademia

Bernardino Luini
School of Milan

Born about 1480—1490, probably at Luino (by the Lago Maggiore), died in 1532 in Milan. He chiefly painted frescoes and altarpieces in Milan and the other towns of Lombardy. In his youth he was influenced by Borgognone, Bramantino and Foppa but this influence was forced into the background by Leonardo's art. Among the host of pupils gathered around Leonardo, Luini and

10 BERNARDINO LUINI:
Study of drapery. Verso of Plate 9

Antonio Solario mutually influenced one another in their art, though the study of the works of Boltraffio, another painter who was considerably older than Luini, has certainly left some traces in the art of the younger artist.

SEATED WOMAN
Verso: STUDY OF DRAPERY

PLATE 9
FIG. 10

204×274 mm. (8″×10¾″). Black chalk, grounded dark pink on yellowed paper. From the Reynolds, Poggi and Esterházy collections. Inv. No. 1881.

Literature
C. Ruland, *The Works of Raphael Santi da Urbino.* London, 1876, p. 328, No. LVI; *E. Hoffmann, 1931*, p. 146, Figs. 16—21; L. Vayer, *Master Drawings.* Budapest, 1957, No. 22; *Velencei . . . rajzok, 1960*, Cat. No. 132.

In the Esterházy collection the drawing was considered Raphael's work. C. Ruland was of the same opinion. But in the Year-Book of the Museum (1931) Edith Hoffmann proved convincingly that the drawing was made by Luini. The head of St. Catherine in the fresco "Martyrdom of St. Catherine," painted by Luini in 1530 in the Church of S. Maorizio in Milan, as well as the heads in the fragments of the frescoes of the Palazzo Rabia in Milan (Berlin Museum)—the head of a nymph in particular (No. 219D)—decisively prove the correctness of Edith Hoffmann's attribution. The sheet in Budapest is a previous contribution to the study of Luini's art as a draughtsman, which has not yet been sufficiently clarified.

Bartolomeo Montagna
School of Vicenza

Born about 1450 in Orzinuovi (by Brescia), died in 1523 in Vicenza. From 1480 on until his death he worked at Vicenza—apart from breaks of varying duration at Verona, Padua, Venice and Bassano—and was the founder and most eminent representative of the art school there. Berenson presumes that he studied under the painters Domenico Morone and Francesco Benaglio of Verona. But Giovanni Bellini, Antonio and Alvise Vivarini, and Antonello da Messina exerted a decisive influence on his art. Andrea Mantegna's brittle style which at the same time conveys a lyricism of expression also made a great impression on him. As Salmi said about him, he belonged "to Brescia by birth, to Vicenza by choice and to Venice by his art."

PLATE 10 THE MADONNA AND CHILD

182×117 mm. (7 1/8"×4 5/8"). Pen, with blue wash. Purchased in 1895. Inv. No. 1780.

Literature
S. Meller, 1911, Cat. No. 117; *E. Hoffmann, 1930*, Cat. No. 72; *E. Hoffmann, Magyar Művészet, 1930*, p. 184; L. Vayer, *Master Drawings.* Budapest, 1957, No. 15; *Velencei ... rajzok, 1960*, Cat. No. 5; *L. Puppi, Arte Veneta, 1959—1960*, Plate 354; L. Puppi, *Bartolomeo Montagna.* Venice, 1962, p. 143, Plate 88.

It was G. Frizzoni who identified this drawing. First Simon Meller and then Edith Hoffmann exhibited it as Montagna's work. The drawing stands close to Montagna's early paintings of the Virgin, such as the painting representing the

Madonna with St. Sebastian, dated 1487, in the Accademia Carrara in Bergamo. It also shows a close affinity to a Madonna from the year 1495, though the latter evinces more plastic forms which are nearer to the style of the high Renaissance. (B. Berenson, *Italian Pictures of the Renaissance.* London, 1957, Vol. I, Plates 496 and 498.) From a stylistic point of view the sheet can be placed among Montagna's drawings without any reservation. As an analogy the sheet No. 597 of the Uffizi Gallery can be referred to. (C. Gamba: *I disegni della R. Galleria degli Uffizi.* Florence, 1914. Scuola Veneta, No. 8.) In its sentiment the head of the Budapest Madonna reminds us of the beautiful head of the Virgin in the collection of the Ashmolean Museum in Oxford, and the much more pictorial effect of the latter can be ascribed to the difference in the techniques of the two drawings. (*K. T. Parker, 1958,* No. 10.) A similar sort of affinity can be found between our drawing and the variant of the Oxford Madonna preserved at Windsor, which served as a study to the Madonna's head in Bartolomeo Montagna's large altarpiece in the Brera, signed and dated 1499. *(Popham—Wilde, 1949,* Cat. No. 19, Plate 7.) The drawing in Budapest has common features with a drawing at the Boymans Museum in Rotterdam, whose attribution to Cima da Conegliano has sound foundations. (*D. v. Hadeln, 1933,* p. 2.) Lionello Puppi in "*Arte Veneta*" establishes a connexion between the sheet in Budapest and the "Pala Cartigliano" by Montagna, painted about 1495.

Gaudenzio Ferrari
School of Lombardy

Born about 1470 at Valduggia in Piedmont, died in 1546 in Milan. He was a pupil of Martino Spanzotti. In Milan he became acquainted with the art of Leonardo and his followers, first and foremost Luini and Bramantino, nevertheless his style remained highly original and individual. He worked at Varallo, Arona, Novara, Morbegno, Vercelli, Como and Saronno, but mainly in Milan. His pictures are characterized by powerful realism and, at the same time, by vigorous passion. In his frescoes the movements of the figures as well as their foreshortening anticipate the achievements of early Baroque mannerist art. His strong personality greatly influenced the Milan masters at the turn of the sixteenth and seventeenth centuries.

THE FOUR EVANGELISTS

PLATE 11

269×188 mm. ($10\frac{5}{8}'' \times 7\frac{3}{8}''$). Brush, bistre, heightened with body-white on yellow prepared paper. From the Esterházy collection. Inv. No. 1854.

Literature

F. Antal, Gaudenzio Ferrari két rajza [Two Drawings by Gaudenzio Ferrari]. *Művészet*, 1915, pp. 331—333; *id.*, Rezension des Buches von Siegfried Weber : Gaudenzio Ferrari und seine Schule. Strassburg, 1927. *Repertorium für Kunstwissenschaft*, 1930, p. 203; Luigi Grassi, Gaudenzio Ferrari e i suoi disegni. *L'Arte*, 1941, p. 205; *Velencei . . . rajzok, 1960*, Cat. No. 131, Plate 3.

In the Esterházy collection the drawing was still specified as 'School of Raphael.' The attribution to Gaudenzio Ferrari is due to Frigyes Antal who dated the drawing as from between 1520 and 1528 and assumed it was made prior to the frescoes of Saronno. The other sheet in Budapest Antal dealt with in his review on Weber, "The Entombment of Christ," which was attributed by Simon Meller to Gaudenzio Ferrari and exhibited by Edith Hoffmann in 1930 with a question mark by Gaudenzio Ferrari's name, is only an inferior imitation of a later date or a compilation after Gaudenzio Ferrari. On the basis of the review by Frigyes Antal in the "*Repertorium*," Luigi Grassi included both of the Budapest sheets in the list of Gaudenzio Ferrari's drawings.

The Budapest drawing of the four Evangelists in its harsh beauty is a fine and remarkable work of the master. In our opinion it is a very late work, contemporaneous with the monochrome painting, very much in the style of a drawing, of "Christ Carrying the Cross" in the Museo Borgogna at Vercelli. The catalogue of the Gaudenzio Ferrari exhibition of 1956 sets the date of this painting at the end of the fourth decade. (*Mostra di Gaudenzio Ferrari*. Vercelli, 1960, Plate 70 and p. 160.) Accordingly the Budapest drawing is to be placed at a date later than the frescoes of Saronno, which Gaudenzio Ferrari was commissioned to do about 1534 and which he, in all probability, had not completed before 1537.

Giorgione, Giorgio da Castelfranco
Venetian School

Born in 1477 or 1478 at Castelfranco, died in 1510 in Venice. He set out from the workshop of Bellini and was influenced by Antonello da Messina's painting, the impressive atmosphere of which had been inspired by the Dutch artists' ideas of space. The art of Carpaccio and Leonardo also exerted an influence on him. By bringing about full harmony between his figures and the landscape surrounding them, he achieved the intimate and deep lyricism characteristic of his works. Contrary to the Quattrocento style, his colours gained a novel meaning and were transformed into elements which created the mood of the picture. He had a decisive effect on Titian as well as on the whole of sixteenth-century North Italian art.

165×113 mm. ($6\frac{1}{2}'' \times 4\frac{3}{8}''$). Pen, bistre. From the Esterházy collection. Inv. No. 1783.

Literature

Schönbrunner—Meder, Albertina Publication, No. 1137; *Tietzes, 1944*, No. 703; Antonio Morassi, Un disegno e un dipinto sconosciuti di Giorgione. *Emporium*, LIX, 1955, p. 158, Note 1; *Velencei ... rajzok, 1960*, Cat. No. 12, Fig. 6; *L. Puppi, Arte Veneta, 1959—1960.*

In the Esterházy collection the drawing was attributed to Hans von Kulmbach (!). In the publication of the Albertina, Schönbrunner—Meder specified it as "Unknown Venetian artist of the sixteenth century." In Edith Hoffmann's handwritten catalogue it figured as the work of a "Venetian artist of about 1500." Its attribution to Giorgione originates from the Tietzes. Although the spirit of Bellini still asserts itself, the drawing, as was emphasized by Tietzes, too, the modelling of the forms has a freer effect, and the composition which is only partly preserved—in its present form the sheet is but a fragment, which is substantiated by the figure cut off from the right side of the drawing—distinctly indicates the trend of Giorgione's art. Tietzes are finding a relationship, which is more than mere chance, with the drawing of a landscape in the collection of S. Schwarz in New York and the Budapest sheet (*Tietzes, 1944*, No. 713). L. Fröhlich-Bum published the New York drawing as Giorgione's work, following Edmund Schilling's oral attribution. (L. Fröhlich-Bum, Venezianische Landschaftszeichnungen. *Belvedere*, 1930, I, p. 86, Plate 65/2.) According to Tietzes Giorgione's hand is particularly seen in the shape of the tree on the right side of the drawing, the placing of the figures and their relationship with the background. Tietze, at this point, refers to the painting "Judith" by Giorgione, which is in the Hermitage in Leningrad. When making his attribution he also takes into consideration the Leonardo-like appearance of the figures and the predilection for half-shades. The way the groups of figures are isolated from one another corresponds to the painting "Madonna in a Landscape" in the Hermitage. In Tietzes' view the Leningrad painting is only a fragment of a horizontal composition, and they presume to see in the Budapest drawing a concept for the composition of the missing half of the painting.

Though in itself the little sketch is unpretentious enough, considering the intimate and lyric expression Giorgione achieved by the unity of the mood of the landscape and the figures, it is within the bounds of possibility that the drawing is the work of his hand. Antonio Morassi, again, made the following remark on our drawing in a note: "*A mio parere, opera del Giambellino verso il 1480.*" The above-mentioned drawing of a landscape from the Schwarz Collection in New York is not considered a Giorgione by Morassi who regards it as of

ture given at the German Institute of Art History in Florence, Geisenheimer declared that they were designs for the frescoes completed in 1597 by Bernardino Poccetti in the former refectory of Sto. Spirito in Florence. (H. Geisenheimer, *Mitteilungen des Kunsthistorischen Institutes in Florenz*, Vol. I. Autumn, 1908, p. 44. Berichte über die Sitzungen des Institutes; A. Gottschewski, *Monatshefte für Kunstwissenschaft*. Rundschau. Florence, 1908, p. 455.) The third sheet mentioned by Longhi, "*Putto dormente*," was identified by the author as a work of the Piedmont artist Guglielmo Caccia detto il Moncalvo and published as such in the Bulletin of the Budapest Museum 1963 (No. 22).

The attribution of "The Nativity" to Romanino can be supported by our investigations, since we succeeded in identifying the painting to which the drawing had served as a preparatory sketch: the large "*Natività*," at the Pinacoteca Tosio e Martinengo in Brescia, a picture that formerly adorned the altar of the church of S. Giuseppe in Brescia (Fig. 11). By this fact the attribution to Romanino has gained a firm foundation. The only major difference between the painting and the drawing is that in the painting the two shepherds are placed behind St. Joseph and in the drawing behind the Virgin. This modification, as against the drawing, sets off the Holy Family much more clearly and makes the whole composition more harmonious and uniform. When creating the painting, Romanino was particularly close to the art of Lorenzo Lotto whose effect is much stronger in the drawing than in the altarpiece at Brescia. In the latter the singular and highly individual lyricism of Lorenzo Lotto could not assert itself fully, since in the silvery and soft texture of the garments the influence of Savoldo makes itself felt, whereas the soaring *putti* betray the effect of Pordenone. The delicate face of the Virgin and the charm of her expression and features in the drawing reflect to perfection the spirit of Lotto. Let us consider another painting of Lotto's, "The Adoration of the Shepherds," which is also to be found at the Pinacoteca of Brescia. The picture, dated 1527 to 1528, is an anticipation, a *terminus post quem* of Romanino's painting "Natività," which he may have painted about 1530. This date also provides a clue to the time when our drawing was made. Among the few of Romanino's drawings considered as authentic we must indicate the red chalk drawing identified by Morassi as a work of the master's and preserved in the Collection Rasini in Milan. (*La pittura bresciana*. Catalogo della Mostra, 1939. Disegni, No. 9.) It is most akin in style to the Budapest sheet. The same style of drawing with its thick, blurred and parallel shading as well as the drapery of the Madonna's garments can be found in Romanino's drawing in the Uffizi Gallery, representing the Virgin between St. Rochus and St. Sebastian. (Uffizi, No. 2113. Cf. C. Gamba: *I disegni della R. Galleria degli Uffizi*, III, 1. Scuola Veneta, No. 15.)

Girolamo Romanino

GROUP OF ARMED RIDERS

PLATE 14

280 × 270 mm. (11″ × 10³/₄″). Pen, bistre on greenish-grey paper. From the Esterházy collection. Inv. No. 1990.

Literature

Schönbrunner—Meder, Albertina Publication, No. 585; L. Fröhlich-Bum, Studien zu Handzeichnungen der italienischen Renaissance. *Jahrbuch der Kunsthistorischen Sammlungen.* Neue Folge, Vol. II. Vienna, 1928, p. 187, Fig. 253; *Tietzes, 1944,* No. A. 387; L. Vayer, *Master Drawings.* Budapest, 1957, No. 37; *Velencei . . . rajzok, 1960,* Cat. No. 13; A. Morassi, *Alcuni disegni inediti del Romanino. Festschrift. Karl M. Swoboda.* Vienna, 1959, pp. 189—192, Plate, 44; *L. Puppi, Arte Veneta, 1959—1960.*

In the publication of the Albertina the drawing was listed as a work of Titian (No. 585). Lilli Fröhlich-Bum considered it to be the work of Paris Bordone from about 1525 and related it to the picture "St. George" in the Vatican. It was Tietze who first mentioned Romanino as the artist. Lajos Vayer published the drawing under the heading "Venetian Artist of the Sixteenth Century." In the publication in honour of Karl M. Swoboda in Vienna, Antonio Morassi published the sheet as Romanino's work, too. He pointed out that it belonged to the most characteristic drawings of the master, had been made about 1530 and might be in connexion with the frescoes at Trento.—In the exhibition of Venetian drawings in Budapest, the sheet was shown as a Romanino (Cat. No. 13). The attributions of Tietze and Morassi are convincing. Comparisons with Romanino's drawings in Berlin (G. Nicodemi, *Girolamo Romanino.* Brescia, 1925, p. 21) and in Oxford (*K. T. Parker, 1958,* No. 26), moreover with the painting "The Tiburtian Sibyl" on the organ shutter at the Cathedral of Asola (Nicodemi, *Girolamo Romanino,* p. 108) and the frescoes in the Colleoni Palace at Malpaga (A. Morassi, The Other Painter of Malpaga. *The Burlington Magazine,* LVIII, 1931, p. 123) exclude the possibility of any doubt. Lionello Puppi agrees with the attribution to Romanino and refers on the basis of information in the *Catalogue of the Exhibition of Venetian Drawings* (Budapest, 1960) also to the frescoes at Malpaga.

Anonymous, Padua or Ferrara, about 1520

A GROUP WITH THE VIRGIN FROM A CRUCIFIXION

PLATE 15

274 × 204 mm. (11″ × 8″). Pen, brush, brownish-grey ink, body-white on yellowed paper. From the Esterházy collection. Inv. No. 1771.

Literature

Paul Kristeller, *Andrea Mantegna.* London, New York, Bombay, 1901, p. 459; *E. Hoffmann, 1930,* No. 25; *Velencei . . . rajzok, 1960,* Cat. No. 9.

In the Esterházy collection the drawing was at first considered a work of Andrea Mantegna's and later of Marco Zoppo's. Paul Kristeller did gainsay the attribution to Mantegna but declared that, in his opinion, the sheet was an inferior work of a later date. In 1930 Edith Hoffmann exhibited the drawing as "Artist of Ferrara, about 1500" (Cat. No. 25). Roberto Longhi termed it "a strange *Pietà* of Padua" and brought it into connexion with the drawing of a *Pietà* attributed to Giovanni Bellini, which is preserved in the Museum of Rennes. (R. Longhi, *Vita artistica,* 1927, p. 138; *Tietzes, 1944,* No. 321.) Later Edith Hoffmann wrote upon the mount of the drawing the name Ercole Roberti with a question mark. It is all the more interesting that Giuseppe Fiocco, who had seen a photograph of the drawing but did not know of Edith Hoffmann's supposition, also thought of Ercole Roberti as the artist. (Oral information, 1959.) Indeed, the drawing in Budapest shows a certain similarity in composition with the painting "The Crucifixion" by Ercole Roberti in the vestry of the Church of S. Petronio in Bologna (F. Filippini, *Ercole da Ferrara.* Florence, 1922, Fig. 30) but it is even nearer to a drawing of Ercole's in Berlin, which shows an even closer affinity with the painting. (L. Grassi, *Il disegno italiano.* Rome, 1956, Fig. 69.) A drawing attributed to Ercole Roberti in the British Museum should also be taken into consideration. (A. E. Popham—Ph. Pouncey, *Italian Drawings in the Department of Prints and Drawings in the British Museum.* London, 1950. No. 229, *verso.*) But side by side with the similarities to Ercole, substantial differences can also be observed. However animated and passionate Ercole may have been, the forceful striving for a diagonal effect, so markedly conspicuous in the drawing in Budapest, cannot be found in his *oeuvre.* This also supports the conjecture that the drawing may have been the work of a generation somewhat later than that of Ercole Roberti.

Correggio, Antonio Allegri

School of Parma

Born between 1489 and 1494 in Correggio, died there in 1534. Probably he was a pupil of Francesco Bianchi Ferrari at Modena. His encounter with Andrea Mantegna's works at Mantua made a deep impression on him, nor was the art of Lorenzo Costa without any effect on him. Present research assumes—as against Vasari—that Correggio must also have stayed for some time in Rome. His art bespeaks the direct influence of Michelangelo's and Raphael's works, and Leonardo's *sfumato* is also alive in his work. His frescoes in the Church S.

Giovanni Evangelista and in the cupola of the Cathedral of Parma belong to the most important works of the High Renaissance. These compositions built upon the effects of illusion and perspective had a decisive effect upon monumental Baroque painting. His drawings are mostly preparatory studies for certain paintings and frescoes. Not a single carefully elaborated '*modello*' is to be found among his sheets.

MADONNA ENTHRONED IN CLOUDS

PLATE 16

Study for the fresco of the "Coronation of the Virgin" in the apse of the Church S. Giovanni Evangelista at Parma. The fresco was painted between 1520 and 1524 but only fragments of it remained. (Exhibited at the Pinacoteca of Parma.)

Pendant of the next drawing.

263 × 183 mm. (10¼″ × 6¼″). Red chalk. From the Houlditch, Hudson, Reynolds, Poggi, and Esterházy collections. Inv. No. 2101.

Literature

E. Hoffmann, *Másolatok, hamisítványok* [Copies and Forgeries]. Exhibition Catalogue. Budapest, 1944, Cat. No. 44; A.E. Popham, Some Drawings by Correggio. *The Burlington Magazine*, March, 1952; A.E. Popham, *Correggio's Drawings*. London, 1957, Cat. No. 26; I. Fenyő, Some Newly Discovered Drawings by Correggio. *The Burlington Magazine*, CI, December, 1959, pp. 421—425; *id.*, Correggio ismeretlen rajzai [Unknown Drawings of Correggio]. *Művészettörténeti Értesítő*. Budapest, 1959, No. 1, p. 1; *Velencei . . . rajzok, 1960*, Cat. No. 134, Fig. 4.

In the Department of Prints and Drawings of the Budapest Museum the drawing, along with the two following sheets, was considered a copy after Correggio. Their extraordinary quality and four engravings published by A.E. Popham in "*The Burlington Magazine*" (1952) which he believed to have been made from lost drawings by Correggio, two of them corresponding with the Budapest drawings, convinced us that the drawings were authentic. One engraving, which corresponds with the Madonna dealt with here, was probably made by the German artist C. M. Metz in the collection of the painter Sir Joshua Reynolds. (A. E. Popham, *Correggio's Drawings*. London, 1957, Fig. 19.) The grandeur and ingenuity of the composition of the Madonna makes it worthy of inclusion among Correggio's most beautiful drawings. The boldness with which the sitting figure is placed, and which determines the sweep of the drapery, is enhanced by the *putti* rushing from all directions to the Virgin's feet where the stream of drapery is brought to a standstill, these features lend the work a vigour that reminds of Michelangelo. The delicate head of the Madonna, bent to the opposite side, produces a contrast which in its soft lyricism and graceful girlish appearance is reminiscent of all the Madonnas and saints of Correggio. The soft curves of the arms crossed at the bosom reveal Michelangelesque fullness and convey in the gracefulness of the movement and in the dreamlike touch of the fingers true Correggiesque tenderness. No copyist could ever have achieved this *élan*, this quality of lightness and suspension.

Our drawing testifies to a close relationship with the famous Correggio Madonna-drawing in the Louvre (A.E. Popham, *Correggio's Drawings.* London, 1957. Cat. No. 26) but it is closer to the fresco than the Paris sheet.

Correggio

PLATE 17 CHRIST ENTHRONED IN CLOUDS
FIG. 12 *Verso:* THE SAME REPRESENTATION

Study for the fresco "The Coronation of the Virgin" in S. Giovanni Evangelista at Parma. Pendant of Plate 16.

245×152 mm. (9⁵/₈″×6″). Red chalk. *Verso:* a variant of the figure of Christ. Red chalk, with pen and brown ink over it. This sheet, too, is cut off on the right-hand side, and thus a part of the garment and of the right arm have been curtailed.—From the Richardson, Hudson, Reynolds and Esterházy collections. Inv. No. 2102.

Literature

I. Fenyő, Some Newly Discovered Drawings by Correggio. *The Burlington Magazine*, 1959; *id.*, Correggio ismeretlen rajzai [Unknown Drawings of Correggio]. *Művészettörténeti Értesítő*, 1959; *Velencei . . . rajzok, 1960*, Cat. No.135; F. Lugt, *Le dessin italien dans les collections hollandaises*. Exhibition Catalogue. Paris, Rotterdam, Haarlem, 1962, Cat. No. 100.

The sheet, too, though formerly considered a copy, is a convincing original, clearly the counterpart of the Madonna discussed before. The same artistic spirit reigns in this sheet, too: the heavy and powerful lower part of the body sets off the graceful trunk which bears an exquisite head with serenely passive countenance. The figure of Christ on the *recto* gives the impression of having been the first design for the fresco. (H. Bodmer, *Correggio und die Malerei der Emilia.* Vienna, 1942, Plate 13.) Although the trunk and the head are quite sketchy, they correspond in their posture with the figure in the fresco. The Christ on the *verso* is more elaborate; the body, the garment and the movements are more distinctly outlined, and the gesture of the hand holding the sceptre is more

12 Correggio: Christ Enthroned in Clouds. Verso of Plate 17

17; L. Vayer, *Master Drawings*, Budapest. 1957, No. 42; I. Fenyő, Some Newly Discovered Drawings by Correggio. *The Burlington Magazine*, 1959, p. 425; *id.*, Correggio ismeretlen rajzai [The Unkown Drawings of Correggio]. *Művészettörténeti Értesítő*, 1959, No. 1; *Velencei... rajzok, 1960*, Cat. No. 136.

Up to quite recently the sheet was considered to be Correggio's work. In three exhibitions of the Department of Prints and Drawings it was displayed by Edith Hoffmann under the name of Correggio. Corrado Ricci, too, treats it as Correggio's work, and it appeared as such at the Correggio Exhibition at Parma in 1935. The attribution of our drawing to Bernardino Gatti is due to A.E. Popham. (Popham, A. E., *Correggio's Drawings*. London, 1957, p. 174.) This attribution is fully convincing. It is enough to cast a glance at Gatti's painting "The Betrothal of St. Catherine" in the collection of the Earl of Yarborough at Brocklesby Park, as well as at the drawing belonging to it, which is in the British Museum and which was identified by Philip Pouncey as a Gatti, to agree with the attribution (Popham, A.E., *Correggio's Drawings*. London, 1957. p. 174, Plates 57 and 59). Gatti's altarpiece "The Adoration of the Shepherds" in the Church of S. Pietro at Cremona also stands very close to the drawing in Budapest. (A. Venturi, *Storia dell'Arte*, Vol. IX, Part VI, p. 822, Fig. 499.) In all the works mentioned above the same egg-shaped head of the Madonna is to be seen, almost a stereotype, with a high forehead and swollen eyelids, similar to that of the sheet in Budapest. In this connexion Gatti's drawing in Windsor should also be pointed out. (*Popham—Wilde, 1949*, Plate 139.)

GIOVANNI BATTISTA FRANCO, CALLED 'SEMOLEI'
Venetian and Roman School

Born in Venice in 1498, died there in 1561. In his youth he found his way to Rome and there was mostly influenced by Michelangelo, Raphael and Giulio Romano. Later he was active in Florence and in other Tuscan towns. 1542 found him again in Rome but by 1554 he had returned to his native town, where he obtained a great number of commissions. In Rome he had been a faithful follower of Michelangelo, in Venice he adjusted himself to the style of Venetian painting. Old sources particularly stress his abilities as a draughtsman. As an engraver, too, he was renowned.

PLATE 20 DESIGN TO A HISTORICAL (?) SCENE

Verso: Sketches of figures

168×278 mm. (6⅝″×10⅞″). Pen. From the Houlditch, Reynolds, Poggi and Esterházy collections. Inv. No. 1869.

Literature

Schönbrunner—Meder, Albertina Publication, No. 715; *Velencei... rajzok, 1960*, Cat. No. 16.

Schönbrunner—Meder first published the drawing as Giovanni Battista Franco's work. This attribution is fully justified when compared with other sheets by him—for example, those in the Albertina in Vienna (Cat. I, 1926) and in the Ashmolean Museum in Oxford (*K. T. Parker, 1958*, No. 19) exhibit the same technique and the same pattern of lines. In Franco's drawings the School of Michelangelo has left its unmistakable traces. Outlines play an important part with him, which is a rare phenomenon among Venetian artists. However, even in Rome the pictorial interplay of lines in Franco's graphic style remained Venetian. (See B. Degenhart, Zur Graphologie der Handzeichnung. *Kunstgeschichtliches Jahrbuch der Bibliotheca Hertziana*, Vol. I, 1937.)

The subject represented is hard to interpret. In the handwritten catalogue of the Museum the drawing is entered under the title "Head of the Vanquished Enemy." The scene "Pompeius' head being handed over to Julius Caesar" can hardly be taken into consideration. There is no principal figure in the composition which could be interpreted as that of Julius Caesar, thus the figures could only be taken for secondary characters. Nor do the garments refer to Roman times. The movement of the central figure is closest to a composition by Antonio Zanchi depicting this particular scene. (Cf. A. Pigler, *Barockthemen*. Budapest, 1956, Vol. II, p. 360.)

Anonymous, Venice, end of the sixteenth century

THE BEARING OF THE CROSS

PLATE 21

194×293 mm. (7⅝″×11½″). Black chalk on greenish-blue paper impregnated with oil and turned brown. From the Mariette, Poggi and Esterházy collections. Inv. No. 1971.

Literature

D. v. Hadeln, *Titian's Drawings*. London, 1929, Plate 21; *E. Hoffmann, 1930*, Cat. No. 83; *id., Magyar Művészet, 1930*, p. 193; *Tietzes, 1944*, No. A 1885; L. Vayer, *Master Drawings*. Budapest, 1957, No. 38; *L. Puppi, Arte Veneta, 1959—1960; Velencei... rajzok, 1960*, Cat. No. 23.

An old inscription on the drawing reads "Tician." Hadeln published the sheet as Titian's work in 1929. Edith Hoffmann listed it in her handwritten

in a crude style, nevertheless it conveys an impression of great strength, movement and dynamism and is thus considered to have been drawn by the artist's own hand.

Follower of Domenico Campagnola

PLATE 23 MOUNTAINOUS LANDSCAPE WITH ANTIQUE RUINS

215×356 mm. (8½"×14"). Pen, light-brown bistre. From the Mariette (Lugt 1852) and Esterházy collections. Inv. No. 1805.

Literature
Schönbrunner—Meder, Albertina Publication, No. 647; *Velencei ... rajzok, 1960*, Cat. No. 25.

In the Esterházy collection the sheet was described as a work of Domenico Campagnola's, and as such it was first published by Schönbrunner and Meder. It was exhibited by Edith Hoffmann at an exhibition of the Department of Prints and Drawings in 1930 (Cat. No. 84) also under the master's name. The drawing does indeed markedly point to Domenico Campagnola's art but the lyric charm characteristic of his landscapes and reminiscent of Giorgione and of Titian is lacking. The conception and the aspect of the landscape, too, suggest a later style, a transition to that of the seventeenth century. In our opinion it was drawn at a period when the Bologna School in particular adopted numerous elements of the approach to landscapes from Venetian art. But the Budapest drawing is only linked to the Bologna School by the common model, and its Northern Italian origin is unquestionable. It is especially the figures of the drawing that are reminiscent of a drawing in the collection of Frits Lugt in The Hague, a sheet mentioned by Tietze under the name of Constantino Malombra. (*Tietzes, 1944,* Plate LXXXI, Fig. 4.) Malombra worked at Padua towards the end of the sixteenth century. Two more drawings published by L. Fröhlich-Bum as Schiavone's works belong to the same group of style. (L. Fröhlich-Bum, *Venezianische Landschaftszeichnungen.* Belvedere, 1930, p. 88, Plate 67/1 and 2.)

After Titian (Domenico Campagnola?)

PLATE 24 LANDSCAPE WITH WOODS AND TOWN

226×335 mm. (8¾"×13¼"). Pen, brown ink on yellowish, faded paper. From the Crozat and Esterházy collections. Inv. No. 1972.

Literature

E. Hoffmann, 1930, Cat. No. 74; *Tietzes, 1944,* No. 1979; F. Klauner, Venezianische Landschaftsdarstellung von Jacopo Bellini bis Tizian. *Jahrbuch der Kunsthistorischen Sammlungen in Wien,* Vol. LIV, 1958, p. 145; *Velencei ... rajzok, 1960,* Cat. No. 22.

In the Esterházy collection the drawing was held to be a work of Titian's. At the 1930 Exhibition of the Department of Prints and Drawings, Edith Hoffmann displayed it as a Giulio Campagnola (Cat. No. 74). Tietzes (*1944,* No. 1979) considered it an early copy after Titian or, at least, a drawing inspired by Titian. In an interesting article Friderike Klauner published it with reservations as a work by Domenico Campagnola. The Budapest drawing shows a close resemblance to another one in the Uffizi Gallery, a sheet published by Carlo Gamba as Domenico Campagnola's work. (C. Gamba, *I disegni della R. Galleria degli Uffizi.* Florence, 1914. Seria Terza, Fascicolo Primo, IX. Scuola Veneta, No. 23.) Tietzes ascribed this drawing to the 'Circle of Titian.' (*Tietzes, 1944,* No. 1988. Cf. also *Tietzes, 1944,* No. 1987.) Reproduced in an article by Odoardo H. Giglioli in *Dedalo.* (O.H. Giglioli, Disegni italiani di paese nella Galleria degli Uffizi. *Dedalo,* 1928—1929, IX, Vol. I, p. 180.)

In the author's view the boldness and lavishness of the composition point to Titian, but only to a copy after him. Owing to the dryness and lifelessness of the execution, however, it can hardly be a work of Domenico Campagnola's.

Anonymous, Venice, sixteenth century (Domenico Campagnola?), with corrections by Rembrandt

HILLY LANDSCAPE WITH HOUSES AND A WATER-MILL

162 × 277 mm. ($6\frac{3}{8}'' \times 10\frac{7}{8}''$). Pen, reworked with brown ink and bistre, and heightened with a little body-white, on yellowish-brown paper. At bottom right an old inscription, scratched out and illegible. From the Esterházy collection. Inv. No. 1579.

Literature

Otto Benesch, *The Drawings of Rembrandt.* London, 1957, Vol. VI, Cat. No. 1369; *Velencei ... rajzok, 1960,* Cat. No. 24, Fig. 8.

On the grounds of the indication in Edith Hoffmann's catalogue, A.M. Hind has stated that the sheet is a Venetian drawing corrected by Rembrandt or another artist of Rembrandt's circle. In his monumental work on Rembrandt's drawings, Otto Benesch devoted to this sheet a whole chapter entitled "Drawings by Other Masters, Reworked by Rembrandt." He ascribes the drawing to Dome-

tion of the painting is to be found in a guide-book of Cremona of 1762, moreover there is an old copy of the painting in the parsonage of Viadana, near Cremona. This altarpiece used to be the finest ornament of the Church of Sta. Maria del Cistello at Cremona and was one of the most famous art monuments of the town.

In its connexion with the painting the Budapest sketch published here gains an extraordinary meaning and importance. Even more intensely than the painting, this drawing radiates the *aura* of Titian's art, the animatedness of the picture being rather a forerunner of early Lombardic Baroque art. The sheet also throws a new light upon Boccaccino as a draughtsman. Up to now only such drawings of his were known upon which the personalities of artists like Correggio, Parmigianino and Pordenone had left their imprints. The sheets in question were even mistaken for the drawings of these three masters. Examples of this style can be found at the Ashmolean Museum at Oxford and in the Louvre (A. E. Popham, *Correggio's Drawings.* London, 1957, p. 133, Fig. 68), as well as in the Bonola Codex of the Museum of Warsaw. (M. Mrozinska, *I disegni di Codice Bonola del Museo di Varsavia.* Catalogo della Mostra, 1959, p. 33, and p. 17 del Codice, No. 1.) Both in these drawings and in his paintings the artist conveys the impression of being the forerunner of the Lombardic art of the early Seicento. In this connexion we have in mind, first of all, Giulio Cesare Procaccini.

UNKNOWN FOLLOWER OF GIORGIONE, ABOUT 1530

PLATE 27 **DANCING FIGURES IN LANDSCAPE**

198×165 mm. (7¾″×6½″). Pen, bistre. From the A. Crozat (?) (Lugt 474) and J. Richardson (Lugt 2170) collections. Inv. No. 58.13 K.

Literature

Velencei... rajzok, 1960, Cat. No. 15; *L. Puppi, Arte Veneta, 1959—1960; id.*, Nota sui disegni del Fogolino. *Arte Veneta, XV*, 1961, pp. 223—227, Fig. 274.

This fine drawing irradiating a specific Giorgionesque atmosphere was found in the Museum in 1958 in the uninvestigated material which had been set aside years before as worthless. In the Exhibition of Venetian Drawings in 1960 the drawing was listed under the above title. On the grounds of a photograph Giuseppe Fiocco considered the sheet—according to oral information—to have been made by the Vicenza artist Marcello Fogolino (active between 1510 and 1548?). When reviewing the Budapest Exhibition, Lionello Puppi in "*Arte Veneta*" accepted Fiocco's attribution and in the next volume of "*Arte Veneta*" presented a detailed study to Marcello Fogolino's drawings, in which he published the

14 PARMIGIANINO: St. Cecilia and David. Organ wing of the Church of Steccata at Parma

sheet in Budapest as this artist's work. His analysis as well as the analogies—with the *verso* of a drawing in Dijon on one hand and the painting "*Concerto*" attributed to Fogolino and preserved in the Museo Civico in Vicenza on the other—seem to be fairly suggestive. In its mood in particular the Vicenza painting is related to our drawing. However, the latter also displays elements alien to Fogolino's art, and that is why we cannot accept the attribution to him as fully convincing.

PARMIGIANINO, GIROLAMO FRANCESCO MAZZUOLA
School of Parma

Born at Parma in 1503, died at Casalmaggiore in 1540. His early style was dominated by Correggio, and he might even have been his pupil. In his early youth he was given important commissions to decorate with frescoes the

Chapels of S. Giovanni Evangelista at Parma; moreover, as testified by an old document dated 1522, he was entrusted to decorate the southern transept of the Cathedral of Parma. He must have painted the graceful frescoes of Rocca di Fontanellato soon afterwards, since in November, 1524, he was already staying in Rome, where the works of Michelangelo, Raphael and Perino del Vaga had an effect on him. In 1527 he, too, was compelled by the *Sacco di Roma* to leave the Eternal City. He turned to Bologna, where he was commissioned with large-scale works by the Church. In 1531 he was commissioned to paint the frescoes for the Church of Sta. Maria della Steccata at Parma. He was one of the founders of the style of mannerism and became one of its most outstanding representatives. He was a brilliant and indefatigable draughtsman who also was the first in Italy to make etchings, and he produced excellent examples in this technique. Parmigianino's effect reached far beyond the frontiers of Italy. Both in France and in Germany traces of his artistic influence can be found.

PLATE 28 ST. CECILIA
PLATE 29 *Verso:* TWO STUDIES OF A DAVID FIGURE

Studies for the paintings on the organ shutter of the Church of Sta. Maria della Steccata at Parma.

291×195 mm. (21½″×7⅝″). Pen and greenish-brown wash. On the *recto* some traces of red chalk and of body-white. From the Lely, Richardson, Poggi and Esterházy collections. Inv. No. 2108.

Literature

I. Fenyő, Some Newly Discovered Drawings by Parmigianino. *The Burlington Magazine*, CV, April, 1963, pp. 145—149, Figs. 1 and 6.

The attribution to Parmigianino was made by the author. The importance of this drawing lies not only in its truly Raphaelesque beauty. To the art historian it is of such particular significance because it is a hitherto unknown study for one of Parmigianino's paintings, namely "St. Cecilia" on the organ shutter of Sta. Maria della Steccata, Parma (Fig. 14). (S. J. Freedberg, *Parmigianino. His Works in Painting.* Cambridge, Mass., 1950, p. 224; G. Copertini, *Il Parmigianino.* Parma, 1932, Vol. I, pp. 36—37; *Inventario degli oggetti d'arte d'Italia.* III. *Provincia di Parma.* Rome, 1934, p. 68.) The only sheet related to these paintings on the organ shutter and hitherto known was a drawing of St. Cecilia in the Louvre *(A.E. Popham, 1953,* 4), where the figure is also shown in reverse direction.

Now the Budapest drawing supports the opinion steadily growing in recent years that the organ shutter in the Steccata is not the work of Bedoli—as has been claimed by some authorities in the past—but of Parmigianino, a view entirely in agreement with existing sources. Regarding the early date of the drawing—before Parmigianino's journey to Rome—see the author's explanations in "The Burlington Magazine." (Cf. also Armando Ottaviano Quintavalle, *Il Parmigianino*. Milan, 1948.)

Not less interesting are the sketches of David on the *verso* of the Budapest sheet. The two musicians, brilliant characterizations, recall modern designs for the figurines of the theatre. They are no less important than the "St. Cecilia" on the *recto*, for they are undoubtedly studies for the other organ shutter of the Steccata. But they differ rather more from the picture than the St. Cecilia figure. It was the latter that provided the clue that led us to the idea of recognizing in these charmingly decorative figures the David of the organ shutter. Without her they would have been very hard to identify. The artist's imagination in these preliminary sketches appeared inexhaustible.

PARMIGIANINO

A WOMAN SEATED AT A TABLE
Verso: TWO FEMALE NUDES

PLATE 30
PLATE 31

183×119 mm. (7¼″×4¾″). Red chalk. From the Praun and Esterházy collections. Inv. No. 2138.

Literature

Christophe Théophile de Murr, *Description du Cabinet de Monsieur Paul de Praun à Nuremberg*, 1797, p. 46; I. Fenyő, Some Newly Discovered Drawings by Parmigianino. *The Burlington Magazine*, CV, April, 1963, pp. 145—149, and Figs. 11 and 13.

In the Esterházy collection the sheet was indicated as Parmigianino's work, and in the early nineteenth century even the name "Parmigianino" was written on it. Later the sheet was denied to have been his and declared to be of Dutch origin, attributable to Cornelisz Bega (!). We consider it to be a typical and extraordinarily beautiful drawing of the great Parma artist.

However surprising the reality of the concept of the portrayal of a woman engrossed in her housework may appear for Parmigianino, the fact is that the representation of various themes of everyday life is not so rare in his graphic art. Drawings of similar genre were published by Popham in his book (1953) about Parmigianino's drawings (Figs. XVIII, XIX, XLII and LXXII). One of the best evidences of Parmigianino's gift for genre scenes is "Old Woman Spinning," engraved after Parmigianino by Enea Vico (Bartsch, XV, p. 301, No. 39) who, in this case, has succeeded in preserving the manner of his great compatriot better than in the rest of his engravings based on the master's work.

These two fine female nudes are truly classic examples of Parmigianino's mature draughtsmanship. The author is inclined to recognize in these girlish

15 Enea Vico: Proserpina.
After Parmigianino. Engraving

figures of graceful bearing studies for the Steccata virgins. The girl on the right, shown in profile with a raised arm, appears to be a sketch for one of the figures on the left of the Steccata ceiling. (*S.J. Freedberg, 1950*, Plate 104.) This opinion is supported by a drawing in Parma, intended for this figure in the Steccata of an exceedingly slender nude girl, whose bearing agrees to a surprising degree with that of the Budapest sheet. (*A.O. Quintavalle, 1948*, Plate 69.) The girl in the Budapest drawing looking at the beholder may well correspond to the central figure in the Steccata group. The dating of the Budapest sheet with the Steccata sketches appears also further justified by the close stylistic link with a magnificent drawing in the British Museum, "A Woman Placing a Garland round the Neck of a Winged Horse." (*A.E. Popham, 1953*, Plate 54.) The *verso* of a further Steccata study at Chatsworth displays a drawing similar in style and subject, "A Nude Woman Fondling a Winged Horse." (*A.E. Popham, 1953*, Plate 58.) It can be assumed that both drawings are of the same date.

Parmigianino

PROSERPINA CHANGING ASCALAPHUS INTO AN OWL

PLATE 32

140 × 94 mm. (5½" × 3¾"). Red chalk. From the Praun and Esterházy collections. Inv. No. 2134.

Literature

Christophe Théophile de Murr, *Description du Cabinet de Monsieur Paul de Praun à Nuremberg*, 1797, p. 46, No. 13 (?); I. Fenyő, Some Newly Discovered Drawings by Parmigianino. *The Burlington Magazine*, CV, April, 1963, pp. 145—149, Fig. 8.

The drawing until very recently among the collection of Italian copies impressed the author with its outstanding quality; he considers it to be the work of Parmigianino's. The composition is known from an engraving of the Parmesan Enea Vico, already mentioned (Fig. 15). (Bartsch, XV, p. 303, No. 45.) A.E. Popham reproduced a small drawing in the British Museum, which to all appearances is an earlier version of the same subject as the Budapest example. (*A.E. Popham, 1953*, Plate 69b.) Our sheet portraying Proserpina displays close stylistical links with the work in the Steccata. At the same time, it recalls a famous drawing in the Uffizi—probably still of the artist's Bologna period—"Circe Bewitching the Companions of Ulysses." (*A.E. Popham, 1953*, Plate 22.)

Parmigianino

TWO MODELS

PLATE 33

140 × 166 mm. (5½" × 6½"). Pen. *Provenance* unknown. Inv. No. 58.105 K.

Literature

I. Fenyő, Some Newly Discovered Drawings by Parmigianino. *The Burlington Magazine*, CV, April, 1963, pp. 145—149, Fig. 7.

This drawing, so strange in its theme, was also found among the mass of anonymous material. It is undoubtedly Parmigianino's work. The drawing is pasted onto a sheet of thicker paper. If held against the light, the figure of a woman exquisitely drawn, as if it were a portrait, becomes visible on the *verso*.

The subject is rather hard to explain. Andor Pigler assumes that it might be a studio scene, probably two models posing. (Oral information.) Rodolfo Pallucchini, having been recently shown the drawing in Budapest, thought that it

by the same hand as the sheet "The Adoration of the Magi" at the Biblioteca Reale in Turin. (Aldo Berini, *I disegni italiani della Biblioteca Reale in Torino.* Rome, 1958, No. 403.)

LELIO ORSI
School of Reggio Emilia

Born in 1511, probably at Novellara, where he died in 1587. He worked as a painter, architect and decorator. In the course of his adventurous life, he was first active mainly at Reggio, then in his native town of Novellara and at Bagnolo. He was in Venice in 1553 but a year later he went to Rome and in 1565 lived in Parma. His works which often seem to be dream-like visions reflect the influence of the great masters of the High Renaissance, in the first place Correggio and Michelangelo. According to a source of the seventeenth century, he was a pupil of Correggio's. He was a most singular artist whose style, in spite of its eclecticism and mannerism, is very personal and original.

PLATE 37 THE CREATION OF THE WORLD

453×353 mm. (17⅞"×13⅞"). Pen. On the back an old inscription, reading: "Lelio da Novelara." From the Praun collection. Inv. No. 58. 1185 K.

Literature
Christophe Théophile de Murr, *Description du Cabinet de Monsieur Paul de Praun à Nuremberg*, 1797, p. 45; E. Panofsky, Artist, Scientist, Genius: Notes on the *Renaissance-Dämmerung*. The Renaissance. A Symposium. *The Metropolitan Museum of Art*, Feb. 8—10. New York, 1952, p. 77 ff.; *Velencei ... rajzok, 1960*, Cat. No. 141; I. Fenyő, Sur quelques dessins italiens du XVIe siècle. *Bulletin du Musée National Hongrois des Beaux-Arts*, No. 19, 1961, pp. 65—68.

Christophe Théophile de Murr indicated the sheet as a work by Lelio da Nuovelara No. 1: "Un grand et beau dessin; à la plume." This drawing, so interesting and remarkable not only for its subject, was discovered a few years ago among drawings that had been put aside in the Museum as 'worthless.' The author recognized that it was a drawing by Lelio Orsi. The explanation of the complicated subject we owe to a paper by Erwin Panofsky on a similar drawing by Lelio Orsi preserved in the Louvre. In the above-mentioned article "Artist, Scientist, Genius: Notes on the *Renaissance-Dämmerung*" Panofsky has given a detailed description of the Louvre drawing "The Creation of the World."

Although this sheet is almost identical with the drawing in Budapest, its style seems to be somewhat more sketchy. Our drawing, more meticulously executed, can be considered a *Reinschrift* of the work and was most likely made for an engraving. In this connexion the reader is referred to the author's article in the Bulletin of the Museum, in which Panofsky's highly remarkable explanations are treated in greater detail. In the same publication Michelangelo's influence, a dominant component of the drawing, has also been discussed more thoroughly. The sheet might be a very late work of the artist's. This dating is also supported by Panofsky who thinks that this extraordinary work was created under the impact of the Gregorian reform of the calendar. In 1582 ten days were deleted from the calendar in order to reset the vernal equinox at March 21st, which was the date of the day of the creation according to a tradition dating back to the Fathers of the Church. By this fact the year of 1582 is given as a *terminus post quem* for the date when the drawing was made.

LELIO ORSI

JOSEPH CAST INTO THE WELL BY HIS BROTHERS

PLATES 38—39

150×506 mm. (5⅞″×19⅞″). Pen, brush, yellowish-brown wash heightened with body-white. From the Praun and Esterházy collections. Inv. No. 2531.

Literature

Christophe Théophile de Murr, *Description du Cabinet de Monsieur Paul de Praun à Nuremberg*, 1797, p. 45; I. Fenyő, Sur quelques dessins italiens du XVIe siècle. *Bulletin du Musée National Hongrois des Beaux-Arts*, No. 19, 1961, pp. 68—72.

This sheet, too, originates from the Praun Cabinet, where it was listed as Lelio da Nuovelara No. 2: "*Joseph est mis par les frères dans un puits. lavé*" Then it came into the Esterházy collection, where it was indicated as a Lanfranco (!). It was formerly among the copies in the collection as a "Copy after a Roman Artist of the Seventeenth Century." There can be no doubt that the drawing is a very characteristic and interesting work by Lelio Orsi. As the space at our disposal does not allow a detailed analysis and artistic evaluation of the sheet, the reader is referred to our explanations in the Bulletin of the Museum.

In its remarkable mood, so tensely wrought with premonition, this *contadinesca* stands very close to Lelio Orsi's drawing in New York, entitled "The Flight into Egypt." (Venturi, *Storia*..., 1933, IX, VI, p. 635, Fig. 384.) This drawing with the scene from Joseph's life is also a late work of the artist, like the drawing "The Creation of the World." The richness of the rendering of the

In two exhibitions of the Department of Prints and Drawings, Edith Hoffmann listed the drawing as a work of Cambiaso's. Later, however, she considered the sheet to be a copy and relegated it to the collection of copies, so rich in copies after Cambiaso. Manning and Suida published the fine drawing as a late work by the master's own hand, made after 1570. The author shares their opinion.

Luca Cambiaso

PLATE 43 **THE LAST JUDGEMENT**

400×294 mm. (15¾"×11½"). Pen, bistre, paper stretched on canvas. From the collections of the Dukes of Modena, then Poggi and Esterházy. Inv. No. 1801.

The drawing is a free copy after Michelangelo's "The Last Judgement." Already in 1930 Edith Hoffmann exhibited it under the name of Cambiaso (Cat. No. 150) and indicated in her handwritten catalogue that the drawing had been identified by Johannes Wilde.

Bernardo Castello
School of Genoa

Born in Genoa in 1557, died there in 1629. He was a pupil of Andrea Semino and of Luca Cambiaso. In 1575 he went to Ferrara, where he made friends with Torquato Tasso and prepared the illustrations to the poet's "*Gerusalemme Liberata*" (1585). Afterwards he settled down in Genoa for good, leaving only to visit Rome and go to Turin for a brief stay in 1604. Giovanni Andrea de Ferrari was one of his numerous pupils. The style of his drawings distinctly shows Luca Cambiaso's influence but their composition is very different from that of his master's sheets.

PLATE 44 **BATTLE SCENE**

138×350 mm. (5½"×13¾"). Pen, bistre, wash. From the Delhaes collection. Inv. No. 1820.

Literature
E. Hoffmann, 1942, p. 13, Fig. 18; *Velencei ... rajzok, 1960*, Cat. No. 147.

The drawing which bears the name "B . ° Castello" written in a later handwriting was published by Edith Hoffmann. The manner of drawing, the angular forms and the playfully simplified delineation clearly show that the sheet was influenced by Cambiaso's drawings with their cubistic effect. The author of the present work agrees with the attribution.

Bernardo Castello

SCENE IN A CAMP

PLATE 45

148 × 270 mm. ($5^{3}/_{4}$″ × $10^{5}/_{8}$″). Pen, bistre, wash. From the Esterházy collection. Inv. No. 1821.

Literature

Edith Hoffmann, 1942, p. 13, Fig. 19; *Velencei ... rajzok, 1960*, Cat. No. 149.

Formerly the drawing was considered Tempesta's work. In 1942 Edith Hoffmann ascribed it to Bernardo Castello. She compared the drawing with the fresco on the ceiling of the library in the Palazzo Scassi at Sanpierdarena, which represents "David before Saul in the Camp." (Venturi, *Storia*..., 1932, IX, V, p. 834.) This analogy is so striking that the drawing in Budapest may even be considered a preparatory sketch to the fresco at Sanpierdarena. In any case, there can be no doubt about the correctness of the attribution.

Tintoretto, Jacopo Robusti

Venetian School

Born in Venice in 1518, died there in 1594. He was perhaps a pupil of Bonifazio Veronese and for a short time of Titian. Obviously he was under the influence of Pordenone's works. Among the early mannerists who had an effect on his art were Parmigianino, Schiavone and Jacopo Bassano. He studied engrossedly Michelangelo's works with whose passionate dynamism he was linked by a deep spiritual affinity. He achieved the highest peaks of art particularly in his later works, to which he imparted a visionary, dramatic character. He exerted an enormous influence on the further development of painting.

STUDY AFTER THE SO-CALLED 'ATLAS'
Verso: A VARIANT OF THE SAME SUBJECT

PLATE 46
PLATE 47

257 × 185 mm. ($10^{1}/_{8}$″ × $7^{1}/_{4}$″). Black and white chalk on blue paper. From the Esterházy collection. Inv. No. 1970.

VERONESE, PAOLO CALIARI
School of Venice

Born at Verona in 1528, died in Venice in 1588. At Verona his masters were Giovanni Francesco Caroto, Antonio Badile and Domenico Brusasorci. From 1555 onwards, he mostly worked in Venice. The artists of Brescia—Savoldo, Romanino and Moretto—but first and foremost the Venetians: Titian and Tintoretto influenced his artistic development. In contrast to the dramatic passion of Tintoretto, Veronese was the unequalled master of festively brilliant representations, throbbing with life. The mighty impulses emanating from his painting effected Rubens, Watteau and Tiepolo, and reached even as far as Delacroix.

PLATE 48
PLATE 49

PLATE 54 PLATE 55

PETER OF AMIENS BEFORE THE DOGE VITALE MICHIEL
Verso: AN ALTERED AND PARTLY TRACED VARIANT OF THE SAME SCENE

140×273 mm. (5½″×10¾″). Pen, grey wash. From the Poggi and Esterházy collections. Inv. No. 2408.

Literature

E. Hoffmann, 1927, p. 138, Figs. 23—25; R. Pallucchini, *Mostra di Paolo Veronese.* Exhibition catalogue. Venice, 1939, Cat. No. 73 and Disegni No. X; *Tietzes, 1944*, No. 2049; L. Vayer, *Master Drawings.* Budapest, 1957, No. 39; *Velencei ... rajzok, 1960*, No. 42, Fig. 9.

PLATE 50

Edith Hoffmann pointed out that the drawing was Paolo Veronese's work and had been made as a study for a painting which in turn provided a design for a tapestry. Along with another piece, the tapestry was destined to hang in the Sala del Collegio of the Palazzo Ducale in Venice. The painting is in the Istituto d'Arte 'A. Passaglia' at Lucca. Both the drawing of Budapest and the painting of Lucca were shown at the Paolo Veronese Exhibition in Venice in 1939. Here the painting was dated between 1576 and 1577. Fra Giovanni Antonio Lorenzini made an engraving after the composition, using as a model a *grisaille* copy of the Florentine painter Francesco Petrucci. Ridolfi himself saw the two paintings for the tapestries in Giuseppe Caliari's house, who—as Ridolfi wrote—was the last heir of the Veronese family. The painting connected with the drawing in Budapest is described by Ridolfi as follows:

"Conserua di più due lunghe tele, che Paolo dipinse per ordine del Senato, che doueuano seruir per tesser arrazzi per lo Collegio; In una apparisce l'atto memorando di Religione fatto dalla Republica, all'hora, che il pio Buglione muouendo le armi per ritorre il Sepolcro dell'humanato Dio dalle mani degli infedeli (per lo cui fine s'erano collegati molti Prencipi e Capitani dell'Europa

master, e.g. "The Scouring of Christ" in the Uffizi Gallery (Inv. No. 13093 A). (*A. Forlani, 1958*, Fig. 22.) On this drawing the inscription "*Jacobi Palma pictoris Venet. 1602*" is probably an autograph. Based on this analogy, the drawing in Budapest may be dated at the turn of the sixteenth and seventeenth centuries.

Palma il Giovane

St. Jerome

PLATE 63

239×197 mm. (9⅜"×7⅞"). Red chalk. From the Reynolds, Poggi and Esterházy collections. Inv. No. 2503.

Literature

I. Fenyő, Dessins inconnus du XVe au XVIIIe siècle. *Bulletin du Musée National Hongrois des Beaux-Arts*, No. 22, 1963, pp. 89—123.

In the Esterházy collection it was considered to be Palma il Giovane's work. Edith Hoffmann rejected this attribution and included the drawing in the stock of copies of the Museum. Because the sheet convincingly bears the characteristics of Palma il Giovane's art, the author identified it as the master's original work. The style of the drawing is particularly closely akin to the artist's paintings. Compared with his other drawings it seems more pictorial, and although we know of hardly any other drawings by Palma's hand executed in such a pictorial manner, this sheet must be considered a characteristic work of his. The analogy closest to it is a signed painting by Palma in the Pushkin Museum in Moscow. (M. Mseriantz, A New Picture by Palma Giovane. *The Burlington Magazine*, LXXII, 1938, p. 38.) From the point of view of the genuineness of our drawing it is interesting and instructive to compare it to a print of "St. Jerome" by Hendrick Goltzius, dated 1596, which he made after Palma's work. (Bartsch 226; Hollstein 311.) In its details Goltzius' print stands closer to the painting in Moscow than our drawing but the type of the saint's head tallies with that of the drawing. The Collection of Drawings in the Hermitage in Leningrad contains a typical drawing by Palma, a sketch in pen and ink, showing St. Jerome. Both in the Leningrad sheet and in the Budapest one the artist restricted himself to representing the figure of the saint and the lion, and to indicating a few rocks. (M. B. Dobroklonsky, *Italian Drawings from the Fifteenth and Sixteenth Centuries in the Hermitage*. Moscow, 1940, Cat. No. 253.)

There is a drawing of Palma il Giovane in the Graphic Collection of the Uffizi Gallery, too, with sketches of St. Jerome and of Mary Magdalene. M. Muraro assumes that this sheet was made in the late 'eighties of the sixteenth century. (*M. Muraro, 1953*, Fig. 13.) The figure of St. Jerome as portrayed in the Moscow painting, kneeling and leaning his head on his hand, occurs in this sheet, too, and together with his surroundings shows a definite resemblance to the red chalk drawing in Budapest.

Only when the present work had been put to press did we receive Konrad Oberhuber's written information about having discovered at the Albertina an etching made by Conrad Metz after our drawing with St. Jerome. The representation is in the reverse, as though seen in a mirror; it measures 269 by 195 mm. (10¾″ × 7¾″), the picture itself being only 232 by 195 mm. (9¼″ × 7¾″). It is inscribed: CM. M. Sc. PALMA JOVINE. (In the Collection of Sir Joshua Reynolds R.A.P.) This etching fully confirms the author's attribution.

Palma's drawings in chalk in most cases differ greatly in technique from his pen and ink drawings which possess the distinct characteristics of a rapidly drawn sketch. It is by no means a matter of chance that meticulously executed drawings, such as the study of a head in the collection of R. von Hirsch in Basle (*Tietzes, 1944*, No. 824) or the fine head of a man at the Ashmolean Museum at Oxford (*K.T. Parker, 1956*, No. 425), are drawn in chalk. Both in the Oxford sheet and in the Budapest one the artist used red chalk, although the exclusive use of this material is very rare with Palma indeed. In the so-called 'Second Set' of the Albertina there is a drawing in red chalk, also representing St. Jerome, a sheet the author considers to have been made by Palma il Giovane himself (No. SV 266. V. II. 111).

PALMA IL GIOVANE

PLATE 65a **THE MIRACLE OF THE LOAVES AND FISHES**
PLATE 64 *Verso:* **PIETÀ AND HEAD OF A BEARDED MAN**

168×445 mm. (6⅝″×17½″). Pen, bistre, wash. On the head of a bearded man on the *verso* also some red chalk. From the Fritz Hasselmann (Lugt 1012) and Rudolf Bedő, Budapest, collections. Purchased in 1957. Inv. No. 57.1 K.

Literature

I. Fenyő, 1958, Figs. 37, 38 and 39; *Velencei ... rajzok, 1960*, Cat. No. 49.

Formerly the sheet was considered to have been made in the workshop of Jacopo Tintoretto. However, both the *recto* and the *verso* are so characteristic of Palma that the attribution to him is fully convincing on mere stylistic grounds. But the author has found a confirmation of his attribution in the pictorial *oeuvre* of the master as well, viz. the painting representing the same subject in the Church Sta Maria del Carmine in Venice (Plate 65b), to which the drawing in

Budapest evidently served as a sketch. The sketch and the painting show substantial similarity but the composition of the former is clearer and better arranged, and in it the representation of the crowd conveys a more concentrated effect. We refer the reader to the author's article in the Bulletin of the Museum in 1958. According to Giulio Lorenzetti the painting in the Church of del Carmine was made towards the end of the sixteenth century. (G. Lorenzetti, *Venezia e il suo estuario.* Rome, 1956.) The date corresponds with the style of the drawing, too, this having been the time when Palma emulated Tintoretto in his composition and atmosphere.

The drawing in Budapest is also related to sheets by Palma, which recent research has dated as of the end of the sixteenth century, such as some drawings at the Albertina (*Albertina, I, 1926,* Nos. 183, 184 and 185) and others at the Uffizi Gallery. (*A. Forlani, 1958,* Cat. Nos. 9, 37 and 53.) Thus we may compare the figure of the Virgin praying on the *verso* of the sheet "The Bewailing of Christ" in Budapest (Plate 64) with the seated female figure at the right-hand side of the sketch preserved in the Winslow and Anna Ames Collection at Springfield, Mo. (Winslow Ames, Two Drawings by Palma Giovane. *Gazette des Beaux-Arts,* 1955, Vol. XLV, p. 171.) The "Pietà" on the *verso* is one of the most moving representations of the theme we know in Palma il Giovane's *oeuvre.* The head of a bearded man, too, bears an expression reminiscent of the magnificent portraits in the artist's paintings. These sketches represent the master in his full power of expression and maturity of style.

Palma il Giovane

ADORATION OF THE MAGI

PLATE 66

145×212 mm. ($5^3/_4'' \times 8^3/_8''$). Pen, bistre, wash. From the Esterházy collection. Inv. No. 1984.

Literature

Velencei... rajzok, 1960, Cat. No. 54.

In the handwritten catalogue of the Museum the drawing figured as the work of a "Venetian Artist of the Sixteenth Century." But the vigour and fluency of the lines definitely point to Palma il Giovane's own hand. The relationship with the paintings he created in the 'eighties of the Cinquecento is striking. The portrait-like and magnificent figure of the king kneeling in the left-hand side of the drawing recalls the majestic portraits in the Oratorio dei Crociferi in Venice, which were made at about the same time. It is also interesting to compare our sheet with the drawing prepared for the same cycle and belonging to the Collection of the Accademia in Venice, depicting the scene of "Christ Appearing to the Doge Ziani and to his Wife." (*D. v. Hadeln, 1926*, Fig. 96.)

ANONYMOUS, VENICE, END OF THE SIXTEENTH CENTURY (ANDREA VICENTINO?)

PLATE 67 THE JUDGEMENT OF PARIS

185×240 mm. (7¼″×9½″). Pen, bistre, wash. From the Esterházy collection. Inv. No. 1993.

Literature
Velencei... rajzok, 1960, Cat. No. 35.

In the Esterházy collection the drawing was attributed to Pietro Liberi. Indubitably it was produced during the late period of mannerism when, parallel with Domenico Tintoretto's dramatic style, a pleasing and soft artistic idiom asserted itself. This style already signified the transition to the Baroque school, one of whose relatively early representatives in Venice was Pietro Liberi.

The close likeness of the Budapest drawing to a sheet by Andrea Vicentino (b. 1542, d. about 1617), "The Flaying of Marsyas," which is at Oxford, is striking. (*Tietzes, 1944*, No. 2229, and *K.T. Parker, 1958*, No. 61.) The Tietzes established a connexion between the Oxford sheet and a small painting attributed to Vicentino, which represents a mythological subject and is preserved at the Museum of Padua.

ANONYMOUS, VENICE, ABOUT 1600

PLATE 68 THE FUNERAL OF A SAINT

452×335 mm. (17⅞″×13¼″). Pen, body-white, indigo wash achieving a *clair-obscur* effect. From the Esterházy collection. Inv. No. 1994.

Literature
Velencei... rajzok, 1960, Cat. No. 55.

Strangely enough H. Bodmer wrote the name of Pietro Liberi on the mount of this highly impressive manneristic drawing which is so typical of the turn of the sixteenth and seventeenth centuries. An inscription written in a hand of about 1800 on the reverse side reads: "Fr. Zuccharo." Although the author could not ascribe this characteristically Venetian drawing to Federico Zuccaro who sojourned in Venice only as a visitor, certain similarities connect it with a sketch of his in the New York collection of Scholz. (*M. Muraro, 1957*, No. 25.) Zuccaro's drawing at the Kupferstichkabinett in Munich entitled "Procession during the Plague with Pope Gregory's Vision of Angels" demonstrates the widely different ways in which this artist depicts a similar subject. (P. Halm, B. Degenhart, W. Wegner, *Hundert Meisterzeichnungen...* Munich, 1958, No. 49.)

The style of the drawing in Budapest is closest to that of Palma il Giovane's and also suggests connexions with Schiavone. Cf. Schiavone's drawing at Windsor "The Apparition of St. Mark." (*D. v. Hadeln, 1926*, Plate 15.) The figures in the background of the funeral procession are strikingly similar to the drawing "The Pope Receives a Sovereign" in the Pomeranian Museum at Gdańsk. Maria Mrozinska links the drawing with Andrea Vicentino and lists it under the heading "Painter of Vicenza about 1600." (*M. Mrozinska, 1958*, No. 15.) In his review of the Exhibition of Venetian Drawings in Polish Ownership in the Fondazione Cini, J. Byam Shaw writes that in his opinion the drawing may originate from Palma. (J. Byam Shaw, Venetian Drawings from Poland at the Fondazione Cini, *The Burlington Magazine*, November, 1958, p. 395.) János Scholz has informed the author orally that he thinks the sheet in Budapest represents "The Conveying of St. John's Body from Alexandria of Egypt to Venice." In this connexion see Jacopo Marieschi's drawing which represents the same scene. (A. Morassi, *Disegni veneti del Settecento nella Collezione Paul Wallraf.* Exhibition Catalogue. Venice, 1959, No. 43.)

Giovanni Battista Trotti, called 'Malosso'

School of Cremona

Born at Cremona in 1555, died at Parma in 1619. He was a pupil of Bernardino Campi. In 1594 he studied the works of Correggio at Parma. He worked in Milan, Lodi, Piacenza and numerous other towns. Certain Venetian elements in his art can be traced back to the influence of Camillo Boccaccino, of Pordenone and Romanino.

ST. HOMOBONUS AND ST. HIMERIUS COMMEND THE TOWN OF CREMONA TO THE PATRONAGE OF THE MADONNA

PLATE 69

151×120 mm. (6″×4¾″). Pen, indian ink, wash. From the Delhaes collection. Inv. No. 1973.

17 MONCALVO: The Birth of the Virgin.
Pavia, Museo Civico

MONCALVO

PLATE 71 THE BIRTH OF THE VIRGIN

216×206 mm. (8½″×8⅛″). Pen with grey wash. The bottom right-hand corner of the *verso* is traced with a lead pencil. From the Reynolds and Esterházy collections. Inv. No. 1860.

Literature

I. Fenyő, Dessins italiens inconnus du XVe au XVIIIe siècle. *Bulletin du Musée National Hongrois des Beaux-Arts*, No. 22, 1963, pp. 89—123.

In the Esterházy collection the drawing was considered to be Parmigianino's work; the attribution to Moncalvo is due to Bernice Davidson. The author ascertained that it was a study for the painting "The Birth of the Virgin" by Moncalvo, in the Museo Civico at Pavia (Fig. 17). Although the painting considerably differs from the drawing, the composition in both is identical. The types of the heads in the very graceful and yet somewhat provincial painting are reminiscent of Solario and Giampietrino. The effect of the Campis is also strong here, particularly that of the artistic idiom of Bernardino Campi whose day-dreaming wistful ladies, painted in a rigid manner with stiff faces and high foreheads, are similar to figures we can find in Moncalvo's altarpieces in the Church of S. Sigismondo and the Cathedral of Cremona, as well as in "The Bewailing of Christ" at the Brera Gallery. (A. Venturi, *Storia*..., IX, VI, Figs. 557, 558 and 564.) In contrast to his paintings the drawings of Moncalvo contain numerous elements of Tuscan and Central Italian art. Side by side with Francesco Salviati's influence, the effect of Battista Naldini also makes itself felt here. Naldini's drawing "The Birth of the Virgin" at the Albertina has a surprising number of features in common with the Budapest sheet which represents the same subject. (*Albertina Catalogue*, 1932, No. 292.) Moncalvo's drawings in Budapest are also akin to two others at the Albertina, which Bernice Davidson also recognized as Moncalvo's work. (*Albertina Catalogue*, 1932, Nos. 160 and 191.) "The Birth of the Virgin" in Budapest is closer to the drawings in Turin representing interior scenes. (*A. Bertini, 1958*, Nos. 240 and 250.)

Giulio Cesare Procaccini
School of Milan

Born in Bologna in 1570, died in Milan in 1625. He was the son and pupil of Ercole Procaccini the Elder. He started his career as a sculptor, and some of his plastic works on the Dome of Milan are known. In his youth he also studied in the Carraccis' workshop in Bologna. Later, in Parma, he became influenced stylistically by Correggio and Parmigianino. From the beginning of the seventeenth century onwards, he seems to have turned increasingly to painting. The first commission he obtained as a painter was for the Cappella del Broletto in Milan in 1605. When he was commissioned in 1610 to paint pictures for the Dome of Milan, representing scenes from the life of St. Charles Borromäus, he was already a well-known artist. His first large-scale work, "The Circumcision," which is at the Pinacoteca Estense at Modena, was created between 1613 and 1616. He was active in Genoa about 1618. Among his contemporaries it was chiefly his brother Camillo Procaccini and Cerano who exerted an influence on him. He preferred drawing with a pen to drawing with chalk. In his pen-drawings he was partial to substituting wash with closely crammed parallel lines, and rich and springy curves, by which he achieved a most animated and vivid effect. His chalk drawings show the same lively playfulness of lines.

18 MORAZZONE:
An Angel Playing Music.
Verso of Plate 76

1962, p. 63) made mention of three scenes from the life of St. Francis Morazzone painted for the second cloister of the Church of Sant'Angelo in Milan and indicated in old sources. The subjects of these pictures were "St. Francis before the Sultan," "The Fire-Ordeal of St. Francis before the Sultan" and "St. Francis Praying." Prior to the Morazzone Exhibition the author sent Mina Gregori a photograph of the second Morazzone drawing (Plate 77) which had already been shown at the Exhibition of North Italian Drawings in Budapest in 1960. Mina Gregori considered it to represent "St. Francis before the Sultan." But if our

19 G. Ferroni's engraving after Morazzone. Cf. Plate 77

supposition proves to be correct, and the drawing discussed now actually belonged to the series of pictures at Sant'Angelo, the sheet, whose photograph was sent to Varese, represents "The Fire-Ordeal of St. Francis before the Sultan" (Plate 77). The author is inclined to think that the drawings in Budapest were made later than 1602—1603, the dates Gregori set for the pictures at Sant'Angelo. (Morazzone Catalogue, 1962, p. 34.) In these sheets the monumentality of the frescoes of Sacro Monte at Orta (about 1617) already makes itself felt; moreover, as against the visionary spirit of the artist's earlier works, the compositions of these drawings are simpler, and are, as it were, painted on the ground of reality. For example, if we compare the "St. Francis before the Pope" of Orta (Morazzone Catalogue, 1962, Fig. 154) with the two drawings in Budapest, we can see that the face of St. Francis is of the same type as in the picture "St. Francis Praying" which is in Orta. (Morazzone Catalogue, 1962, Fig. 155.) The fine figure of the music-making angel on the *verso* also speaks for a later date. This angel already points to the music-making angels in the frescoes of Novara, which were made later than the frescoes of Orta. So striking is the resemblance that one may well assume that the drawing was a sketch to the angel playing the violin, in Novara. (Morazzone Catalogue, 1962, Fig. 200.)

MORAZZONE

PLATE 77 THE FIRE-ORDEAL OF ST. FRANCIS BEFORE THE SULTAN

327×243 mm. ($12\frac{7}{8}''\times 9\frac{1}{2}''$). Pen, brown ink, wash, on brownish-yellow paper. From the Delhaes collection. Inv. No. 57.23 K.

Literature

Velencei... rajzok, 1960, Cat. No. 153; M. Gregori, *Il Morazzone. Catalogo della mostra.* Varese, Milan, 1962, pp. 34, 157 and 163, Fig. 23.

In 1960 the drawing was exhibited in Budapest as Morazzone's work. Mina Gregori published in her catalogue an engraving made in 1723 by Girolamo Ferroni for Giuseppe Pozzobonelli, after the frescoes Morazzone had painted for the cloister of Sant'Angelo in Milan. These murals have been since destroyed (Fig. 19). The engraving is almost completely identical with the drawing. As already mentioned, Gregori called this scene "*San Francesco davanti a Sultano.*" We assert that the scene "*San Francesco tra le fiamme*"—"The Fire-Ordeal of St. Francis"—is represented here, a scene which was also depicted by Morazzone at the cloister of Sant'Angelo.

GIOVANNI BATTISTA MAURO DELLA ROVERE,
CALLED 'IL FIAMMENGHINO'
School of Lombardy

Born in 1561, probably in Milan, died there in 1628 (?). Together with his brother Gian Mauro della Rovere who was fifteen years his junior, he fulfilled large-scale commissions for frescoes. 'Fiammenghino' is a representative of the so-called 'Neo-Gaudenzio-Ferrari' style. He as well as his brother produced numerous frescoes both in Milan, and in the towns and villages in the vicinity. Which one of the two brothers painted them, is a problem still to be solved. Their graphic style is also so utterly blended that defining their individual *oeuvre* as draughtsmen is a task set before art schools.

MOSES, ABOVE HIM A PUTTO WITH A BOOK AND A SERPENT

PLATE 78

287×103 mm. (11¼″×4″). Bistre, wash, body-white, on blue paper. From the Esterházy collection. Inv. No. 2359.

Philip Pouncey, who identified the drawing on the basis of a photograph, did not know that the dated initials of the artist, "J.B.R.18.MR 1628," were written on the reverse side of the sheet in the same ink. The inscription not only bears witness that the drawing is the elder brother's work but also that Giambattista Mauro della Rovere was still living in 1628. The sheet is of such high artistic quality that it proves that the master, who was of the same age as Camillo Procaccini, belonged, together with Cerano, Giulio Cesare Procaccini and Morazzone, to the most eminent exponents of Lombardic graphic art.

Stylistically our drawing is related to several sheets at the Ambrosiana in Milan. (E. Spina Barelli, *Disegni di maestri lombardi del primo Seicento.* Exhibition Catalogue. Milan, 1959, Nos. 76 and 77 with illustrations.) Moreover, it plays an important role in separating the style of the two brothers in the stock of drawings in that collection. Carrying out this task is rendered easier by the circumstance that two published sheets of the Ambrosiana bear the monogramme (and the date of 1636) of the younger della Rovere.

Giovanni Battista Mauro della Rovere

CHRIST APPEARING BEFORE HIS DISCIPLES

PLATE 79

200×375 mm. (7⅞″×14¾″). Bistre, wash, body-white, squared in red chalk on brown paper. From the Poggi and Esterházy collections. Inv. No. 2402.

In the Esterházy collection it was ascribed to Giulio Campi. However, the attribution to Giovanni Battista Mauro della Rovere is based on a comparison of this drawing with the preceding one (Plate 78) as well as on stylistic similarities with other drawings by him. In the sheet "The Resurrection of Christ" the face of Christ is of the same type. (E. Spina Barelli, *Disegni di maestri lombardi del primo Seicento.* Exhibition catalogue of the Ambrosiana Collection. Milan, 1959, No. 71.) The drawing is also akin to the sheet listed under No. 79 in the same catalogue as well as to No. 80, which is rounded off with a semi-circle. However, among the sheets by Fiammenghino in the Ambrosiana, our sheet is most closely related to "The Wedding in Cana," a work evidently influenced by Morazzone's style. (Ambrosiana Cat., 1959, No. 83.) Another drawing by Giovanni Battista della Rovere, "The Prodigal Son," to which the author refers in making his attribution, is in the "*Codex*

Bonola" in the Museum of Warsaw. (M. Mrozinska, *I disegni del Codice Bonola del Museo di Varsavia. Catalogo della mostra.* Venice, 1959, p. 54, pagina 26, Cat. No. 23 with a figure.) The resemblance between the type of face with a long and pointed nose, which it portrays, and the profile of the Apostle kneeling on the stairs in the Budapest sheet is astonishing. Even more interesting is a comparison of the latter with a drawing by G.B. Fiammenghino in the Dome of Milan, that the artist made for the cycle of St. Charles Borromäus. (M. Gregori, Ricordi figurativi del Manzoni. *Paragone*, No. 9, 1950, Fig. 3.) Compare the type and the carriage of the head of the youth standing beside the door with that of the man hurrying away, but looking back at Christ in the Budapest sheet. Here again a worthy task is offered to Italian art historians who are proficient in della Rovere's *oeuvre* to ascertain whether the Budapest drawing is connected with any of his frescoes.

MARCANTONIO BASSETTI
Schools of Verona and Venice

Born in Verona in 1558, died there in 1630. The most diverse tendencies merge in his art. In Verona he studied under Felice Brusasorci. Jacopo Tintoretto exerted a great influence on him, but mainly through the medium of the art of his student Palma il Giovane. The effects of the Bassano workshop also make themselves felt in his style. In 1616 he went to Rome, where his interest was aroused by Michelangelo da Caravaggio. He came into direct contact with Saraceni. His style also shows links with Orazio Borgianni. Nor did Fetti's pictorial richness fail to have an effect on him. Bassetti was only a year older than Fetti, and numerous links connect his painting style with that of the great innovator of Mantua. His drawings, however, are characteristic products of North-Italian—Venetian late mannerism. Only recent research has succeeded in delineating his personality.

PLATE 80 MOSES STRIKING WATER FROM THE ROCK

209×271 mm. (8¼"×10⅝"). Brush drawing in bluish mauve, with plenty of body-white. *Provenance* unknown. Inv. No.58.8 K.

Literature
Velencei... rajzok, 1960, Cat. No. 36; *L. Puppi, Arte Veneta, 1959—1960*; I. Fenyő, Dessins inconnus du XVe au XVIIIe siècle. *Bulletin du Musée National Hongrois des Beaux-Arts*, No. 22, 1963, pp. 89—123.

The author based his attribution on Bassetti's drawings at the Windsor collection, which had been identified as this artist's works by A.E. Popham (quoted by A. Blunt and E. Croft-Murray, *Venetian Drawings... at Windsor Castle.* London, 1957, p. 25), who in his attribution again depended on Bassetti's drawing "*Sta. Pudenziana e Sta. Prassede*" preserved in the Bernasconi-Signorelli Collection and published by Roberto Longhi. (R. Longhi, *Precisioni nelle Gallerie Italiane. I. Reale Galleria Borghese.* Rome, 1928, p. 63.) In 1959 Longhi again investigated Bassetti, and the two pictures of the Sala Regia of the Quirinal, which he published, fully confirm the correctness of Popham's attribution of the Windsor sheets. (R. Longhi, Presenza alla Sala Regia. *Paragone*, 1959, No. 117, p. 29, Figs. 5a and 5b.) The two frescoes published by Longhi also support the attribution of the Budapest drawing.

Bassetti's graphic style is quite close to Saraceni's. Suffice it to refer to the latter's drawing "The Assumption" at the Biblioteca Ambrosiana in Milan. (L. Grassi, *Il disegno italiano.* Rome, 1956, Fig. 150.) Bassetti worked beside Saraceni in the Church of Sta. Maria dell'Anima in Rome (the paintings of this church have been destroyed), which partly explains the affinity of their art as draughtsmen.

Otto Benesch found a sheet representing "The Miracle of the Loaves and Fishes" among the Dutch drawings of the Albertina and identified it as Marcantonio Bassetti's work. (Oral information.) (Reproduced by I. Fenyő, *Bulletin...*, No. 22, 1963.) This drawing is closely related both to the one in Budapest and to those at Windsor. *(Blunt—Croft-Murray, 1957*, Nos. 1, 7, 16, 17.) Strangely enough the *versos* of both the Vienna and the Budapest sheet bear the name "Barth. Flamael" written in pencil in a hand of the nineteenth century. In both instances this name is completely unjustified, since the style of Bertholet Flamael, an artist born at Liège and active about the middle of the seventeenth century, is absolutely different from the style of either drawing. According to written information received from János Scholz, one Bassetti drawing in his collections bears also the inscription "Barth. Flamael."

Domenico Fetti (?)
School of Mantua

Supposedly born in Rome in 1589, died in Venice in 1623. Cigoli was his master but the art of Caravaggio and of the German Elsheimer had an even greater influence on his style. From 1613 on he was the court painter of the Gonzagas in Mantua. In 1621 he went to stay in Venice, and the art of the City of the Lagoons made so deep an impression on him that he settled down and worked there until his untimely death. The effects of Tintoretto, Bassano and Veronese

wards he worked in Venice. At the same time two of his fellow-artists, Fetti of Mantua and Jan Lys of Holstein, settled down there. They formed the great tripartite constellation of painters whose artistic achievements were based on the traditions of the Venetian Cinquecento—particularly on Veronese—and it was they who handed down these attainments to the great artists of the seventeenth and eighteenth centuries.

PLATE 83 CHRIST AND THE WOMAN OF SAMARIA

165×168 mm. (6½″×6⅝″). Pen and bistre, wash. From the Esterházy collection. Inv. No. 1848.

Literature
I. Fenyő, Contributo ai rapporti artistici tra Palma Giovane e Bernardo Strozzi. *Acta Historiae Artium*, 1958, p. 143, Fig. 2; V. Moschini, Inediti di Palma il Giovane e compagni. *Arte Veneta*, XII, 1958; *Velencei... rajzok, 1960*, Cat. No. 61; *L. Puppi, Arte Veneta, 1959—1960*, Fig. 356.

Because of an inscription of a later date, the sheet was ascribed in the Esterházy collection to Lodovico Carracci. Victor Lazareff agreed with the author's attribution to Strozzi (oral information), and so did L. Puppi in "*Arte Veneta.*" The drawing is closely related to the composition of a painting of the same subject by Palma Giovane, which is in Genoa (I. Fenyő, *Acta Historiae Artium*, 1958, p. 143, Fig. 2) but it is done in a more advanced style than Palma's. Comparing the drawing with other works of Strozzi's, particularly his paintings, it is evident that it must be his work. Through this interesting link between the art of Palma Giovane and that of Strozzi, it is highly instructive to observe the elements pointing towards the Baroque in the works of the mannerist Palma on the one hand, and on the other the manneristic reminiscences in Strozzi's art. The theme of "Christ and the Woman of Samaria" was painted by Strozzi several times. Closest to the Budapest drawing is his painting at the Kasteel Weldam in Holland. (L. Mortari, Su Bernardo Strozzi. *Bollettino d'Arte*, 1955, IV, Catalogue of the Paintings, p. 330.) The painting, irradiated by sunshine, is a fine example of Strozzi's *preveneziano* style—the manner in which he worked in the years before he left Genoa.

BERNARDO STROZZI

PLATE 84 CHRIST IN THE HOUSE OF SIMON

188×303 mm. (7⅜″×12″). Pen, bistre, body-white, wash on blue paper which has faded into greenish-grey. From the Poggi and Esterházy collections. Inv. No. 2393.

Literature

E. Hoffmann, 1942, pp. 14—15, Figs. 20, 21; L. Mortari, Su Bernardo Strozzi. *Bollettino d'Arte*, 1955, IV, p. 326, Foot-note 29; I. Fenyő, Contributo ai rapporti artistici tra Palma Giovane e Bernardo Strozzi. *Acta Historiae Artium*, 1958, p. 149, Figs. 5, 6; *Velencei ... rajzok, 1960*, Cat. No. 59.

As testified by an inscription on the mount dating from the beginning of the nineteenth century, the drawing was also registered as Strozzi's work while still in the Esterházy collection. Edith Hoffmann adopted this attribution and pointed out the connexion between the drawing and the large painting of the same subject, which is in the Academy in Venice. (*E. Hoffmann, 1942*, pp. 14—15.) In his article written in 1926 on Genoese painters, Delogu mentioned that a *bozzetto* of the Strozzi painting "Christ in the House of Simon" in Venice had first belonged to the Cambiaso family in Genoa and later to the Collection Montarsolo there. (G. Delogu, Pittori Genovesi del '600. *L'Arte*, 1926, p. 180.) This *bozzetto* of Genoa, which is now privately owned in Florence, was published by Anna Maria Matteucci in 1955. (A.M. Matteucci, L'attività veneziana di Bernardo Strozzi. *Arte Veneta*, 1955, p. 138.) She also set forth that not only the *bozzetto*, but the painting itself which is preserved at the Accademia in Venice originated in Genoa, which confirms the dating of the sheet in the artist's Genoese period.

Some researchers call the attribution to Strozzi doubtful. Professor Lasareff who had the opportunity to see the original drawing in 1962 is one of them. The author, however, accepts Edith Hoffmann's attribution—which is supported by tradition—as correct. The style, the elements of form as well as the types of the figures, all speak for Strozzi's hand, and the drawing—in spite of its size being different from that of the painting—conveys the impression that it had been made as a sketch to the picture. In the author's opinion the date of the drawing in Budapest can also be set at the last years the artist spent in Genoa. As the colours of the paintings became deeper and warmer at that time, so the manner of the drawing also grew softer—nearly pictorial—and the manneristic interplay of lines observed in earlier drawings had vanished.

Johann Carl Loth, called 'Carlotto'

Schools of Munich and Venice

Born in Munich in 1632, died in Venice in 1698. His father, Ulrich Loth, who had studied in Italy under Carlo Saraceni was his first master. Carlotto was still a youth when he went to Vienna and later to Italy. In about 1660 he first worked in Pietro Liberi's workshop in Venice, then in Florence, Milan and Verona. He then finally settled down in the City of the Lagoons. His art was particularly

PLATE 86 CLEARING IN A FOREST WITH A SLEEPING MAN

195×202 mm. (7⅝″×8″). Red chalk. From the Lugt 1468 and Delhaes collections. Inv. No. 2823.

Literature

Velencei... rajzok, 1960, Cat. No. 60; *L. Puppi, Arte Veneta, 1959—1960;* I. Fenyő, Dessins italiens inconnus du XVe au XVIIIe siècle. *Bulletin du Musée National Hongrois des Beaux-Arts*, No. 22, 1963, pp. 89—123.

In a handwriting of about 1800 "Carpioni" is inscribed on the reverse side of the sheet. Edith Hoffmann included it in the stock of drawings as a "Copy after an Italian Artist of the Eighteenth Century." On the basis of its technique, especially the method of shading with parallel lines and the general effect of the representation, we are convinced that the drawing is Carpioni's work. In the case of this drawing and the following one Lionello Puppi accepts the attribution to Carpioni.

GIULIO CARPIONI

PLATE 87 A SHEET OF SKETCHES WITH BACCHANTES, A RIVER-GOD, THE MAGDALENE(?) AND OTHER FIGURES

268×175 mm. (10⅝″×6⅞″). Red chalk. From the Lugt 2680 (?) 1468 and Delhaes collections. Inv. No. 2824.

Literature

Velencei... rajzok, 1960, Cat. No. 58; I. Fenyő, Dessins italiens inconnus du XVe au XVIIIe siècle. *Bulletin du Musée National Hongrois des Beaux-Arts*, No. 22, 1963, pp. 89—123.

In the handwritten catalogue of the Museum the drawing is listed as by an "Italian Copyist, Eighteenth Century." However, the drawing has no features characteristic of a copy, but is an incontestable creation of the seventeenth century. It speaks for Carpioni's hand. Moreover it is a characteristic work and one of his most beautiful drawings. In explaining our attribution we refer first of all to the drawing "The Heliads at Phaeton's Tomb" in the Albertina (Cat. 1926, No. 225) and to "The Betrothal of St. Catherine" at the Ashmolean Museum in Oxford (*K.T. Parker, 1958*, No. 74).

Antonio Zanchi (?)
School of Venice

Born at Este (Padua) in 1631, died in Venice in 1722. He was a pupil of Francesco Ruschi's. Luca Giordano conveyed to him the influence of Neapolitan art (Ribera) but he was also related to Langetti's style. Apart from Venice, his paintings are to be found at Este, Treviso, Rovigo, Padua, Bergamo, Genoa and many other towns. In Hungary two of his signed large paintings are preserved at Pannonhalma.

ALEXANDER THE GREAT BEFORE THE BODY OF DARIUS — PLATE 88

198×274 mm. (7¾″×10¾″). Pen, grey wash. *Provenance* unknown. Inv. No. 58.82 K.

The monogram "S. R." on the drawing evidently should mean Sebastiano Ricci but to consider him the master of the drawing is out of the question. At the Exhibition of Venetian Drawings in Polish Ownership, held at the Fondazione Cini in Venice, there was a drawing exhibited under the name of "Paolo Pagani," which at once made the author think of the drawing in Budapest. (M. Mrozinska, *Disegni veneti in Polonia.* Catalogue of the Exhibition. Venice, 1958, Cat. No. 21.) The same drawing from Poland was shown at the 1959 Seicento Exhibition in Venice and was ascribed to "Francesco Ruschi." (See the excellent catalogue of the drawings written by T. Pignatti, No. 64.) According to the catalogue the attribution originates from Michelangelo Muraro. The Roman Francesco Ruschi was—as is known—Zanchi's master, and thus it is the more interesting that on the basis of a photograph, Nicola Ivanoff considered the drawing in Budapest to be Zanchi's work. (Oral information.) This may explain the relationship between the drawing in Budapest and the one in Poland.

Pietro Liberi
School of Venice

Born in Venice in 1614, died there in 1687. In the course of his adventurous life he made an appearence in most countries of Europe. According to written sources, Varotari was his master. In his early artistic period he set Titian as his example but the art of his contemporary Sebastiano Mazzoni also had a conspicuous effect on his art. He was commissioned to do large-scale works in public buildings, first of all in the Palazzo Ducale in Venice, but in Padua and Bergamo, too, he painted altarpieces and ceilings. In his later works, side by side with the influences of Pietro da Cortona, those of Luca Giordano are evident.

The magnificent drawing, of very high artistic value indeed, belongs to a series of four studies of heads. See also the following drawing as well as Figs. 22 and 23. In the Esterházy collection the drawings were considered to be Baroccio's. Edith Hoffmann dated them as of the second half of the sixteenth century.

ANONYMOUS, NORTHERN ITALY (MILAN?), BEGINNING OF THE SEVENTEENTH CENTURY

PLATE 91 HEAD OF A BISHOP

376×288 mm. (14¾″×11⅜″). Brush, indian ink, black and red chalk, body-white. From the Esterházy collection. Inv. No. 1842.

Literature

E. Hoffmann, Magyar Művészet, 1930, Figure on p. 199; *Velencei... rajzok, 1960*, Cat. No. 148. Cf. with Plate 90.

GIOVANNI BENEDETTO CASTIGLIONE, CALLED 'GRECHETTO'

School of Genoa

Born in Genoa in 1610 (?), died in Mantua in 1695. He first studied under Giovanni Battista Paggi, then under Giovanni Andrea de Ferrari. In addition to the art of the painters of his native town (Strozzi, de Ferrari) he also became acquainted with the works of the Dutch artists who worked there. In the period between 1639 and 1661 he was in the service of the Gonzagas in Mantua as court painter. Then he again lived in Genoa for a few years and then went to Mantua, where he spent the last years of his life. The art of Poussin, Bernini and Pietro da Cortona in Rome and that of Domenico Fetti in Mantua made a deep and lasting impression on him but his sojourns in Venice, Bologna and Naples also influenced his art. He painted religious and mythological subjects, genre-pictures, still-lives and portraits and was one of the most eminent animal painters of his period. He was a markedly individual draughtsman and often made use of oil-paint in his drawings. His remarkable etchings show the effect of Rembrandt's graphic art. At the same time he appears in this technique as an early forerunner of Tiepolo.

PLATE 92 ALLEGORY IN HONOUR OF THE DUCHESS OF MANTUA

455×332 mm. (17⅞″×13″). Brush, reddish-brown oil paint, blue and white body colours on yellow paper. From the Poggi and Esterházy collections. Inv. No. 2296.

Literature

E. Hoffmann, 1930, Cat. No. 145; *Velencei... rajzok, 1960*, Cat, No. 155, Fig. 15.

Edith Hoffmann supposed the drawing to have been made as a study for an "Adoration of the Shepherds," a favourite subject of Castiglione. Indeed, the Budapest drawing shows an affinity with such compositions; nevertheless it is a quite different representation, an allegory of the same kind as that of the drawing in the Windsor collection.

Anthony Blunt has not only elucidated Castiglione as a draughtsman from new points of view in an article of fundamental importance, in the "Journal of the Warburg and Courtauld Institutes," but has also established a fully convincing chronological order of his *oeuvre* of drawings, mainly by including the paintings and those drawings of the artist which were intended for reproduction. Blunt has supplemented the results for his research work in the exemplary catalogue of Castiglione's drawings at Windsor with still further, new conclusions. In both works he published three drawings of the Windsor collection, which assisted us in identifying the subject of the Budapest sheet. (A. Blunt, The Drawings of Giovanni Benedetto Castiglione. *Journal of the Warburg and Courtauld Institutes*, VIII, 1945, pp. 161—174; *id.*, *The Drawings of G.B. Castiglione and Stefano della Bella at Windsor Castle.* London, 1954, Cat. Nos. 132, 141 and 223.) Both the drawing at Windsor and the one in Budapest are closely related to a painting which was formerly in the Pellicioli Collection, under the traditional title "*Marte e la Duchessa di Mantova col figlio sotto le spoglie di Giunone.*" (G. Delogu, Pittori Genovesi del '600. *L'Arte*, 1929, p. 175.) Assuming that the title is correct, it is—according to Blunt—Maria Gonzaga, Duchess of Mantua and widow of Carlo Gonzaga, who is seated on the right side of the composition; in her lap is her son Carlo who in 1637 inherited the title Duke of Mantua from his grandfather. Until 1647 Maria Gonzaga was Regent for her son. Seated on a pile of weapons on the left, is the so-called Mars with a trumpet in his hand. Blunt is of the opinion that this figure is more a representation of something like Fame or the Genius of Arts and Sciences, and he finds in the Duchess' figure a resemblance to the figure of Ceres. In the hair of the Duchess in the Windsor sheet, there is a garland of flowers which is not depicted in the Budapest drawing. In the middle there stands an old man who—in the drawing at Windsor—has a globe at his feet. According to Blunt the drawing may have been made about 1648, since the figure of 'Mars' is in close relation to the famous etching "The Genius of Castiglione" which bears the date 1648. (Bartsch, 23.) It is easy to imagine that the Duchess ordered a painting of the subject in 1648 when the peace of Westphalia put an end to the wars in which Mantua had suffered so gravely. The exact meaning of the allegory is not clear but—according to Blunt—the composition is identical with the one Baldinucci saw in

1654 and which he called "The Allegory in Honour of Charles I." There the background represents the mausoleum of the late Duke, in front of which the Duchess is seated with her son in her lap.

By setting the date of the drawing at Windsor, the date of the Budapest sheet has also been established. The author presumes that the Budapest drawing was made somewhat earlier than the one at Windsor. In its more spacious and clearer composition the latter tallies with the arrangement of the figures in the painting, whereas the drawing in Budapest still shows the influence of an earlier composition, "The Adoration of the Shepherds." (A. Blunt, *The Drawings of G.B. Castiglione and Stefano della Bella at Windsor Castle.* London, 1954, No. 102, Plate 16, and Cat. No. 131, Plate 23; Cf. also the drawing with "The Adoration of the Shepherds," published in the *Albertina, VI, 1941*, Nos. 518—519.)

Giovanni Benedetto Castiglione

PLATE 93 THE ASSUMPTION OF THE VIRGIN

475 × 358 mm. ($18\frac{3}{4}'' \times 14\frac{1}{8}''$). Red, brown, blue and grey oil-paint. Pen and wash on pale yellow paper. From the Poggi and Esterházy collections. Inv. No. 2297.

Literature

E. Hoffmann, Magyar Művészet, 1930, Figure on p. 197; A. Blunt, *The Drawings of G.B. Castiglione and Stefano della Bella at Windsor Castle.* London, 1954; P. Halm, B. Degenhart, W. Wegner, *Hundert Meisterzeichnungen aus der Staatlichen Graphischen Sammlung.* Munich, 1958; *Velencei ... rajzok, 1960*, Cat. No. 157.

Edith Hoffmann published the drawing in 1930. In the Catalogue of Castiglione's drawings at Windsor, Anthony Blunt published a relatively early pen and bistre drawing of the same subject, which was made between 1640 and 1645 (Windsor Catalogue, 1954, No. 23, Fig. 12), and some late brush drawings of the same subject, which can be dated between 1655 and 1660 (Windsor Cat., Nos. 157, 158 and 159, Fig. 21). Describing the composition as the "familiar Baroque formula," Blunt traces it back to the Carraccis. (Blunt, A., The Drawings of Giovanni Benedetto Castiglione. *Journal of the Warburg and Courtauld Institutes. VIII*, 1954, p. 171.) In connexion with the drawing at Windsor listed under Cat. No. 159, Blunt refers to the drawings in Budapest and Munich. B. Degenhart, too, mentions the Budapest sheet in connexion with the one in Munich (1958).

In his preface to the Catalogue of Windsor, Blunt explains that in 1650 two important sources of Castiglione's style were Bernini and Rubens; moreover

24 G.B. CASTIGLIONE: Figure of a Frightened Man in two variants. Verso of Plate 94

that Castiglione established ties with another native of Genoa, Baciccia, who rendered Bernini's style into a more popular artistic idiom in Rome. Added to these effects was the strong influence of Van Dyck, in whose studio—according to Soprani—Castiglione had studied; and these effects may be discerned both in the drawing in Budapest and in the drawings at Windsor representing "The Assumption." Thus the date of the drawing in Budapest can be set at the same time as that of the Windsor sheets, i.e. between the years 1655 and 1660.

GIOVANNI BENEDETTO CASTIGLIONE

A SHEET OF SKETCHES — PLATE 94
Verso: FIGURE OF A FRIGHTENED MAN IN TWO VARIANTS — FIG. 24

231×328 mm. (9⅛″×12⅞″). Pen, brush bistre. On the *verso* also lead pencil. From the Esterházy collection. Inv. No. 2298.

even if not written on the drawing by the artist himself, seems to be very appropriate. Ligozzi died in 1626 when the Duke was only sixteen years of age. Thus, in all likelihood, it was Ansaldo who made both the drawing and the painting." She compared the style of the drawing with that of Ansaldo's painting "The Baptism of the Three Holy Kings" at the Oratorio delle Cinque Piaghe in Genoa and detected in the heavy and thick-set figures a style analogous with the authenticated painting by Ansaldo.

Bartolomeo Biscaino
School of Genoa

Born in Genoa between 1632 and 1636, died there in 1657. He was a faithful follower of his master, Valerio Castello, but Pellegrino Piola, Gioacchino Assereto and Giulio Benso also influenced him. In the course of his short life he chiefly painted altarpieces. As an etcher he followed in Castiglione's tracks.

PLATE 97 THE MADONNA AND CHILD

170×138 mm. (6⅝″×5½″). Red chalk, body-white on yellowish-brown paper. From the Esterházy collection. Inv. No. 2281.

Literature
Velencei... rajzok, 1960, Cat. No. 160.

The traditional attribution is supported by a comparison with the artist's drawings in Vienna (*Albertina, VI, 1941*, Nos. 345—349) as well as by a study of Biscaino's, "The Finding of Moses," at the Palazzo Bianco in Genoa both of which show a very close relationship with the Budapest sheet in style and technique. (Cf. O. Grosso, A. Pettorelli, *I disegni di Palazzo Bianco.* Milan, 1910, No. 39.)

Anonymous, Venice, beginning of the eighteenth century (Andrea Celesti?)

PLATE 98 ESTHER BEFORE AHASUERUS

427×285 mm. (16⅞″×11¼″). Pen, brown wash. Squared. From the Delhaes collection. Inv. No. 2764.

L i t e r a t u r e
Velencei... rajzok, 1960, Cat. No. 72; *L. Puppi, Arte Veneta, 1959—1960.*

Formerly the drawing was specified as "Italian Artist of the Eighteenth Century." The author considers it to be Venetian. In solving the problem of the composition, the artist was undoubtedly influenced by a painting of the same theme by Jacopo Tintoretto, which is at Hampton Court. (R. Pallucchini: *La Giovinezza del Tintoretto.* Milan, 1950, Fig. 189.) It is a well-known fact that in the first half of the eighteenth century the works of the great artists of the Venetian Cinquecento were often copied. Paolo Veronese, in particular, served as an eternal model but Giannantonio Guardi—who so often transposed the paintings of his contemporaries into the harmonies of his own art—also made faithful copies, e.g. of Jacopo Tintoretto's works. (A. Morassi, Antonio Guardi ai servigi del Feldmaresciallo Schulenburg. *Emporium,* April, 1960, pp. 147—163, Figs. 13—16.)

According to the author the composition of the drawing in Budapest, but even more so the types of figures, are reminiscent of Andrea Celesti (1637—1712). For comparison's sake it is sufficient to look at the latter's picture in Dresden, "The Israelites Collecting their Jewels to Cast the Golden Calf." (*Seicento Catalogue.* Venice, 1959, No. 207.) As far as the composition is concerned, there is another painting by Celesti, representing "Christ before Caiphas," in the collection of Gino Calligari at Terzo d'Aquileia, which is also close to the Budapest drawing. (*Seicento Catalogue.* Venice, 1959, No. 213.)

We know but little of Celesti's art as a draughtsman. Pignatti's Catalogue of the drawings shown at the 1959 Exhibition in Venice, of which mention has been made, is particularly important in this connexion. Celesti's drawing "David with the Head of Goliath" in Antonio Morassi's collection in Milan shows a certain resemblance to the sheet in Budapest. (*Seicento Catalogue.* Venice, 1959, Disegni, No. 83.) The ragged, *staccato* outlines of that drawing, on the other hand, already testify to the early Rococo style. Should the drawing really be the work of Celesti's own hand—quite independently from the author, Nicola Ivanoff, too, recognized this relationship (oral information)—the conclusion can be drawn that the artist, who by date of his birth belonged to the High Baroque, was influenced during the late phase of his art by the style of a much younger generation—the graphic art of a Sebastiano Ricci and a Giovanni Antonio Pellegrini. Moreover the drawing in Budapest is closely related to a large-size painting of "Esther before Ahasuerus" at the Picture Gallery in Athens, which was published by Emil Waldmann as Andrea Celesti's work. (Emil Waldmann, Die athenische Bildergalerie. *Zeitschrift für Bildende Kunst,* 1912, p. 88. Fig. 7.) But even Waldmann leaves the question open as to whether Andrea Celesti "was the master ... or perhaps once again the Proteus Luca Giordano, after all." Particularly striking is the resemblance between Salome in a painting by Andrea Celesti at the Villa Battoni at Bogliaco and Esther in the drawing in Budapest. (Mucchi e Della Croce, *Il pittore Andrea Celesti.* Milan, 1954, Figs. 27 and 28.)

Here we should like to refer to Carlo L. Ragghianti's Catalogue entitled *Disegni dell'Accademia Carrara di Bergamo*, 1963. It contains an exquisite Venetian drawing on Plate C. representing Esther before Ahasuerus and is attributed to Andrea Celesti with a question mark (Cat. No. 251). From the *oeuvre* catalogue of the book by Mucchi and Croce we know that Celesti painted the story of Esther in the Villa Rinaldi Barbini at Asola (Treviso).

Sebastiano Ricci

School of Venice

Born at Belluno in 1659, died in Venice in 1734. He first studied under Francesco Cervelli in Milan, then under Sebastiano Mazzoni in Florence and finally under Giovanni Giuseppe dal Sole in Bologna. In Bologna, Parma, Rome and Milan he was given significant commissions. He spent the first decade of the eighteenth century in Venice, Vienna and Bergamo. In 1712, as a famous artist, he went to England. In 1717 he travelled through the Netherlands and France and returned to Venice, there to settle down for good. His art was of pioneering significance for the unfolding of Venetian painting in the eighteenth century. Having commenced from the pictorial High Baroque style of the seventeenth century and then having been influenced by the eclectic artists of Bologna, and by Pietro da Cortona and later by Luca Giordano, interesting reciprocal effects developed between his art and that of his famous contemporaries Pellegrini and Magnasco. He directed his interest more and more towards the great traditions of the Venetian Cinquecento. In particular he regarded the festive and magnificent paintings of Paolo Veronese as his examples. G.B. Tiepolo, too, learned from Sebastiano Ricci but his own sweeping power in turn made an impression on the older artist.

PLATE 99 HERCULES AT THE CROSS-ROADS

294×202 mm. (11½″×8″). Pen, brownish-grey wash, a little body-white, traces of pencil on dark grey paper. *Provenance* unknown. Purchased in 1958. Inv. No. 58.1177 K.

Literature

I. Fenyő, 1959, p. 87, Fig. 1; *Velencei . . . rajzok, 1960*, Cat. No. 65.

On account of the satyr-like appearance of the man in the drawing, it was for a long time difficult for us to decide whether the subject of the sheet was

"Hercules at the Cross-Roads" or not. The explanation as such is due to Andor Pigler who pointed out certain details which set the identification of the theme beyond doubt, such as the overturned wine-jug at the left-hand side of the composition as well as the lion's head in the middle—although it is very schematically drawn. With respect to the attribution to Ricci, several drawings of his at the Windsor collection must be referred to. (*Blunt—Croft-Murray, 1957*, Cat. Nos. 216, 231, 275, 292, 345 and 387.) Particularly convincing is a comparison with the drawing representing St. Romuald (Cat. No. 345, Plate 36). The expressiveness of the lines, which are sometimes quite thick and then again very thin, and which here and there end in small hooks and little semi-circles, is identical. For more detailed explications see the author's article of 1959. Furthermore reference should be made to Ricci's frescoes painted in 1706 in the Palazzo Marucelli in Florence, where the artist represented the same subject. (Carlo Gamba, Sebastiano Ricci e la sua opera fiorentina. *Dedalo*, V, Vol. II, 1924—1925, pp. 289—314, Fig. on p. 303.) Although the compositions differ, the same spirit is evident in the conception of the subject, and the proportion of the figures and the gestures are so characteristic of Ricci. We also point to the painting of the Palazzo Marucelli "Youth at the Cross-Roads" in which the artist depicted a subject closely related to the drawing in Budapest, and here again the conception of both works shows a close affinity. (Joachim von Derschau, *Sebastiano Ricci.* Heidelberg, 1922, Fig. 42.)

Next to the collection at Windsor the Accademia in Venice is the richest treasury of Ricci's drawings. Among the 133 drawings by him in the Folio-Volume of the Accademia, there are numerous studies that stand very close to the one in Budapest, which can therefore be included in Ricci's *oeuvre* of drawings without question. A direct connexion with a painting of Ricci's cannot be established. Although the master chose the same theme for an early painting for the Palazzo Bartoldi at Belluno, which was dated by Joachim von Derschau as between 1695 and 1701, the conception here is even more different than that of the work in the Palazzo Marucelli. (Derschau, *op. cit.*, p. 57.) Derschau and later Pallucchini, too, pointed out the Seicento character of this painting and emphasized that the scheme of the composition originated from Annibale Carracci. However, in the Budapest drawing the constraint of the composition appearing in the earlier interpretations of the same subject has disappeared, and the balance of the composition no longer depends on the carefully measured arrangement of the figures. The degree, in which the artist was interested in the balance of the structure of the composition which is already typical of the Rococo, is revealed in the triangle of the foreground. Of course, this is not a triangular composition in the sense of the Renaissance, since the figures are depicted in more animated attitudes, through which are evident certain endeavours for diagonal effects which strongly contrast with the close form of a triangle.

At G.A. Pellegrini's exhibition staged at the Fondazione Cini in Venice in 1959, it was highly interesting to observe how close some of his drawings paralleled Sebastiano Ricci's style; particularly the drawing at the Museo Correr, representing "The Judgement of Paris" (A. Bettagno, *Disegni e dipinti di Giovanni Antonio Pellegrini*. Exhibition Catalogue. Venice, 1959, No. 105), which bears an amazing resemblance to the drawing in Budapest, and which originates from the Diziani material of the Museo Correr. The author considers this drawing to be a work made by Gaspare Diziani in his youth when he was still strongly influenced by Sebastiano Ricci, but also by Pellegrini. Thus the problem connected with it does not only belong to the Pellegrini—Diziani group of problems, as expounded by Bettagno in his catalogue, but raises the much more important question of the connexion between Ricci, Pellegrini, Diziani and even Fontebasso.

GIOVANNI BATTISTA MARCOLA
School of Verona

Born in Verona about 1711, died there in 1780. He made altarpieces for numerous churches of his native town and also worked at Modena. Contemporaneous writers reported that he also painted some 'funny' pictures with small figures. He was the father of the painter Marco Marcola.

PLATE 100 ST. FRANCIS BEFORE THE SULTAN

387×280 mm. (15¼″×11″). Pen, greenish-brown wash. Purchased in 1960. *Provenance* unknown. Inv. No. 60.4 K.

Literature

I. Fenyő, Dessins italiens inconnus du XVe au XVIIIe siècle. *Bulletin du Musée National Hongrois des Beaux-Arts*, No. 22. Budapest, 1963, pp. 89—123.

Signed at the bottom right "G. Batta. Marcola." A sheet in the collection at Bassano, the "Adoration of the Magi" (Licisco Magagnato, *Catalogo della Mostra di Disegni del Museo Civico di Bassano*. Venice, 1956, No. 81) evinces the closest stylistic relationship with our drawing. In Licisco Magagnato's catalogue the Bassano drawing is specified as a work by Marco Marcola (1740—1793) who was the son of Giovanni Battista Marcola. Michelangelo Muraro, however, in the catalogue of the 1957 Venice Exhibition of the Scholz Collection ascribed to the father the drawing at Bassano, along with another one in the Scholz Collection (No. 88), and referred to another drawing of Giovanni Battista Marcola's, which is at the Art Institute in Chicago and was published by Ulrich Middeldorf. (U. Middeldorf, Un disegno di G. B. Marcola. *The Prints Collector Quarterly*, 1940.) Unfortunately this publication has not been available to the author. Another drawing in the Rasini Collection in Milan, "The Adoration of the Shepherds," published by Antonio Morassi under Marco Marcola's name (A. Morassi, *Disegni antichi della Collezione Rasini in Milano.* Milan, 1937, Plate CX) also belongs closely to this stylistic group. The signed drawing by Giovanni Battista Marcola in Budapest may perhaps contribute to distinguishing the style of the drawings of father and son. (Cf. also *M. Mrozinska, 1958,* Cat. No. 72.—A. Bettagno, *Disegni veneti del Settecento.* Catalogo della mostra. Venice, 1963. No. 46.)

Girolamo Brusaferro
School of Venice

Born in Venice in 1700, died there in 1760. He was a pupil of Nicolò Bambini's. As contemporary writers reported, he followed in the tracks of Sebastiano Ricci. He trained himself, moreover, by studying Luca Giordano's art. In addition to Venice he also worked at Rovigo, Padua and Mantua.

THE HOLY FAMILY APPEARING TO ST. STEPHEN

PLATE 101

265×141 mm. (10⅜″×5½″). Pen, bluish-grey wash. From the Wiesböck (Lugt 2576) and Delhaes collections. Inv. No. 58.19 K.

Literature
I. Fenyő, 1959, Fig. 54, pp. 126—127; *Velencei . . . rajzok, 1960,* Cat. No. 66.

The inscription on the drawing identified by the author, "G. Brusaferro," is probably the artist's signature. (*I. Fenyő, 1959,* p. 126.) Zanetti writes that this not too significant artist "*tento anche di far sua la maniera di Sebastiano Ricci.*" The sheet in Budapest shows that these efforts were not fruitless. The drawing, very beautiful in its composition, testifies to the strong influence of Ricci. At the Venice Exhibition of the Scholz Collection of New York (1957) there was a drawing by the master (Cat. No. 87), which bore Girolamo Brusaferro's name written in Zanetti's (?) hand. In the Albertina there is a drawing entitled "Death of a Saint" (*Albertina, I, 1926,* No. 341), which is inscribed in a similar manner. Both the drawing of the Scholz Collection and that in Vienna correspond in style as well as in quality with the sheet in Budapest.

30 Gaspare Diziani: Aeneas and Anchises. Venice, Museo Correr

The manner in which the two sheets are drawn is also very similar. Of course, this similarity is not decisive in distinguishing the two artists, since both may have been drawn by Pellegrini. In our opinion it is indispensable, in trying to solve the questions that may emerge in this connexion, to thoroughly investigate the material of the Städelsches Kunstinstitut. Recently the author was requested by the Board of the Frankfurt Museum to undertake this interesting work, and he hopes that in the course of his investigations this complex of questions can also be resolved.

Reverting to the drawing the "Fighting Knights," its connexion with Gaspare Diziani's large-scale painting "The Massacre of the Innocents" in the Church of S. Stefano in Venice must be considered, particularly with regard to the group in the left-hand side of the foreground (Fig. 28). Together with an article of fundamental importance, the painting was published by Giuseppe Fiocco in 1927. (G. Fiocco, Aggiunte di Francesco Maria Tassis alla guida di Venezia di Anton Maria Zanetti. *Rivista di Venezia*, 1927.)

As already pointed out, the style of the drawing is in close kinship with that of Pellegrini. It is very interesting that a similar motif is to be found in the style of Pellegrini, too, although the resemblance is not so strong with him as it is with Diziani's painting at S. Stefano, wherein we see a warrior treading underfoot a woman who has collapsed on the ground in the centre of the composition entitled "Il terrore della guerra." (R. Pallucchini, Modelli di Giannantonio Pellegrini. *Arte Veneta*, VII, 1953, p. 107, Figs. 97, 98.) At the same time the similarity of the motifs throws a light upon the differences between the artistic personalities of the two draughtsmen. On the other hand, the group in the painting at S. Stefano irradiates the same spirit as our drawing the "Fighting Knights."

GASPARE DIZIANI

AENEAS AND ANCHISES
Verso: A MAN WITH A DAGGER

PLATE 110
FIG. 29

260×333 mm. (10¼"×13⅛"). Pen, washed with indian ink, red chalk, on yellowish, faded paper. From the Lugt 1468 and Delhaes collections. Inv. No. 1651.

Literature

E. Hoffmann, 1930, Cat. No. 220; *I. Fenyő, 1959*, p. 55, Figs. 8, 9; *id.*, *1960*, Fig. 2.; *Velencei ... rajzok, 1960*, Cat. No. 78.

Identified by Edith Hoffmann, this drawing which, particularly in its manner of depicting the landscape, evinces such a markedly Pre-Guardi character, is nearest in style to Diziani's "Fighting Knights" (Plate 109). The robust figure of a man on the *verso* of our sheet is an almost exact replica of a figure in the painting in the Church of S. Stefano "The Massacre of the Innocents" (Fig. 28) already mentioned. Thus it serves in place of a signature in the attribution of our drawing. The author has found a variant of "Aeneas and Anchises," similar in quality to the Budapest sheet, in the collection of the Museo Correr. (Fig. 30 and *I. Fenyő, 1960*, Fig. 2.) Both of the drawings in question contain numerous elements pointing to the so-called "Self-Portrait of Pellegrini" in Frankfurt. The drawing in Budapest is also closely connected with the sketch "A Bishop in Glory" at the Scholz Collection in New York. (A. Bettagno: *Disegni e dipinti di Giovanni Antonio Pellegrini*. Venice, 1959, Cat. No. 81.)

GASPARE DIZIANI

THE RAISING OF THE YOUTH OF NAIN

PLATE 111

223×399 mm. (8¾"×15¾"). Pen, brown wash, red chalk. Acquired in 1916. Inv. No. 1916-15.

Domenico Tiepolo. Hamburg, 1910, Fig. 292; Giuseppe Fiocco, La Pittura Veneziana alla mostra del Settecento. *Rivista della Città di Venezia,* 1929, p. 63; G. Lorenzetti, *Cà Rezzonico.* Venice, 1936, p. 73, No. 15 and Fig. 93; Giorgio Vigni, *Note sull'attività del Tiepolo a Madrid e a Würzburg e sul Quaderno Correr. Venezia e l'Europa. Atti del XVIII. Congresso Internazionale di Storia dell'Arte.* Venice, 1956, p. 163, Figs. 273 and 274.—The drawing in Budapest is a preliminary study for the standing figure of a young man who emerges dominantly in the foreground of the fresco. A relief and a hammer—the symbols of sculpture—are placed at his feet. This figure was formerly believed to be the sculptor Wolfgang van de Auwera but H. v. Freeden has proved that it could not have been intended to represent him after all. H. v. Freeden and Carl Lamb—founding their surmise on a statement of Dr. Othmar Metzger—are inclined to recognize in the figure of the young man the excellent Venetian sculptor Antonio Bossi, who worked at Würzburg and produced the stuccoes and wall figures of the *Kaisersaal.* He also executed the figures of giants in the staircase, which were designed by Tiepolo. (M.H. von Freeden, Ein Würzburger Künstlerbildnis. *Mainfränkische Zeitung,* 1944, 2, II; *id.* and C. Lamb, *Das Meisterwerk des Giovanni Battista Tiepolo. Die Fresken der Würzburger Residenz.* Munich, 1956, p. 95.)

Giovanni Battista Tiepolo

PLATE 120

STUDY

192×138 mm. (7½″ × 5½″). Pen, wash. Presented by Simon Meller in 1932. Inv. No 1932-2341.

Literature

E. Hoffmann, *Legszebb külföldi rajzok* [The Most Beautiful Foreign Drawings]. Exhibition Cat., No. 78; *Velencei ... rajzok, 1960,* Cat. No. 84.

Pendant of the next sheet (Plate 117). (See explanations there.)

It is an unused study related to the ceiling frescoes in the throne room at the Royal Palace in Madrid, made between 1762 and 1764, and entitled "The Glorification of Spain."

Giovanni Battista Tiepolo

PLATE 121

A STUDY FOR THE FIGURE OF THETIS

195×140 mm. (7⅝″×5½″). Pen and wash. Presented by Simon Meller in 1932. Inv. No. 1932-2342.

Literature
E. Hoffmann, 1930, Cat. No. 78; L. Vayer, *Master Drawings.* Budapest, 1957, No. 94; *Velencei ... rajzok, 1960*, Cat. No. 86.

Pendant of the previous sheet. The drawing is a study for the fresco "The Glorification of Spain" made between 1762 and 1764 on the ceiling of the throne room of the Royal Palace in Madrid. It is a detail of the "Oceanus and Thetis" group. (Cf. A. Morassi, *G.B. Tiepolo.* London, 1955, Plate 87.) Of the rich treasures of the sea Thetis offers Spain a shell filled with pearls.

In the author's view this drawing—along with the preceding one—originates from Giovanni Battista Tiepelo's sketch-book entitled "*Sole Figure per Soffitti*," which was taken to pieces and sold only in the nineteen-twenties. Eckhart Knab points out that the new sheets acquired by the Albertina in 1923 and 1925 also originated from this sketch-book. (Eckhart Knab, Rezension über das Buch von George Knox "Catalogue of the Tiepolo Drawings in the Victoria and Albert Museum." *Österreichische Zeitschrift für Kunst und Denkmalpflege*, 1960, XIV, Vol. 4, pp. 140—147.) All the figures in this sketch-book have an incredibly suggestive effect in common, obtained by foreshortening, which conveys a strong impression that they are floating weightlessly in the air. (*Albertina, I, 1926*, Nos. 289—295 and Nos. 298, 299.)

The fact that Tiepolo used the study of Thetis in the throne room of the Royal Palace in Madrid does not contradict its origin of his sketch-book which according to its style must have been made while he was still in Italy. In a letter dated 13th March, 1762—probably addressed to Tomaso Giuseppe Farsetti—Tiepolo wrote that he had nearly completed the design of the throne room: "*Al presente sono al fine del Modello della Gran Opera, ch'è tanto è vasta, basta solo riflettere, ch'è di cento piedi ...*" The full contents of the letter are cited by Pompeo Molmenti. (P. Molmenti, *G.B. Tiepolo.* Milan, 1909, pp. 26—27.)

Giovanni Domenico Tiepolo
School of Venice

Born in Venice in 1727, died there in 1804. He was the son of Giovanni Battista Tiepolo and Cecilia Tiepolo, Francesco Guardi's sister. Already before 1740 he was active in the workshop of his father. As his father's assistant he accompanied him to Würzburg in 1751—1753 and also went with him about a decade later—1762—on his great journey to Madrid. From 1783 to 1785 he worked in Genoa. The frescoes in some of the rooms at the Villa Valmarana by Vicenza (1757) are linked with his name. These works, but especially the brilliant frescoes of the Villa Zianigo, the family residence of the Tiepolos, evince his great talent

32 GASPARE DIZIANI (?): Minerva.
Venice, Museo Correr

31 GASPARE DIZIANI: The Assumption of the Virgin.
Budapest, Museum of Fine Arts

Literature

I. Fenyő, 1959, Fig. 35; *Velencei ... rajzok, 1960*, Cat. No. 120.

This study and the following one (Plate 124b) were among the drawings of the Museum of Fine Arts in Budapest, which had been set aside as worthless. We identified them as Fontebasso's works and published them as such in 1959.

Notwithstanding the differences in size, form and paper of the two drawings they seem to be counterparts; their style shows that they were undoubtedly made by the same hand. The various types on the sheet keep on reappearing in Fontebasso's paintings, e.g. in the series of pictures at Trento and in the large pictures in Budapest. (A. Morassi, Francesco Fontebasso a Trento. *Bollettino d'Arte*, XXV, 1931—1932, p. 123; A. Pigler, Un gruppo di dipinti di Francesco Fontebasso a Budapest. *Arte Veneta*, XIII—XIV, 1959—1960, pp. 155—161.)

Francesco Fontebasso

A SHEET OF STUDIES WITH THE HEAD OF A BEARDED MAN AND TWO HANDS

PLATE 124b

277×187 mm. ($10\frac{7}{8}'' \times 7\frac{3}{8}''$). Black chalk. From the Lugt 2347 and Delhaes collections. Inv. No. 58.79 K.

Literature

I. Fenyő, 1959, Fig. 36; *Velencei ... rajzok, 1960*, Cat. No. 118.

Like the previous one (Plate 124a) this drawing, too, is done with chalk. Up to now scarcely any chalk drawings by Fontebasso were known. In 1954 J. Byam Shaw published in "*Arte Veneta*" a drawing which is in the Museo Correr, entitled "St. Joseph and the Infant Christ," wherein black chalk is dominant over the pen work. (J. Byam Shaw, The Drawings of Francesco Fontebasso. *Arte Veneta*, VIII, 1954, Fig. 316.) In its forms and lines as well as in the manner of the application of the chalk this sheet is exceedingly close to the drawing in Budapest. Suffice it to study the way the hands are drawn! The large hands with long fingers, on which the several joints are drawn with strong emphasis, continually recur in the artist's paintings, too. Not long ago Antonio Morassi published a drawing in black chalk, which bears the signature "Fontebasso" and which is also related to the two chalk drawings in Budapest. (A. Morassi, *Dessins vénitiens du dixhuitième siècle de la collection du Duc de Talleyrand.* Milan, 1958, Fig. 48.) A pen drawing in the collection at Bassano, allegedly representing Metastasio and ascribed to Fontebasso by Fiocco and Pignatti, is also reminiscent of the study in Budapest. (L. Magagnato, *Catalogo della mostra di disegni del Museo Civico di Bassano.* Venice, 1956, No. 70.)

33 GIUSEPPE BAZZANI: The Raising of Lazarus. Whereabouts unknown

MARCO RICCI
School of Venice

Born at Belluno in 1676, died in Venice in 1729. In his early youth he went to Venice and became a pupil of his uncle Sebastiano Ricci. He was found guilty of manslaughter for killing a gondolier and was forced to spend four years in exile at Spalato. Then—after a short stay in Milan—he became Sebastiano Ricci's collaborator in the latter's workshop. The year 1708 found him in London where, working with Giannantonio Pellegrini, he made stage designs. In

1711 he was again in Venice but in the following year back again in London, this time together with Sebastiano Ricci. Subsequently he sojourned in Holland, in Paris and Rome but finally he settled down in Venice for good.—In his landscapes he reflected the heroic *genre* of Salvator Rosa; and among his older contemporaries Alessandro Magnasco exerted a strong influence on him. Later he showed a predilection for the landscapes of the artists of Bologna and of Claude Lorrain. At that time he most frequently made gouache-paintings—often on leather and parchment—whereas his pen-drawings were relatively rare.

LANDSCAPE

PLATE 128

282×401 mm. (11⅛″×16″). Pen. *Provenance* unknown. Inv. No. 2479.

Our attribution to Marco Ricci is based, first and foremost, on the closest relationship of this sheet with a drawing at the Ashmolean Museum. (*K.T. Parker, 1958*, Cat. No. 75.) But in the Windsor collection, so rich in Marco Ricci's drawings, there are numerous parallels to the Budapest sheet. (*Blunt—Croft-Murray, 1957*, Cat. No. 98.) Similar motifs occur in his etchings, too, and so does the characteristic interplay of lines and the manner of shading. (R. Pallucchini, Studi Ricceschi. Contributo a Marco. *Arte Veneta*, IX, 1955, p. 171, Fig. 187.)

BERNARDO BELLOTTO, CALLED 'CANALETTO'
School of Venice

Born in Venice in 1720, died in Warsaw in 1780. He studied in the workshop of his uncle Antonio Canale. Between 1740 and 1745 he stayed in Rome and in several North Italian towns. In 1757 he went to Dresden, where he became court painter of Saxony. Between 1759 and 1760 he sojourned in Vienna. In 1761 he was in Munich but from 1762 to 1767 he again lived in Dresden and from 1767 onwards in Warsaw, until his death. In all these cities he painted a great many series of *vedute*. Bellotto's paintings are less colourful than those of Antonio Canale, and the form-dissolving effect of the atmosphere is not so strongly felt in them. The landscape is mostly suffused by a yellowish-grey, cold light. Bellotto endeavoured to a considerable extent faithfully to render the topography of his *vedute*, and the details of his paintings are astonishing in the way he was able to convey the 'feel' of substance and a closeness to reality. Some Italian writers seem to have observed in his works a certain '*oltramontana pedanteria*.'

As a draughtsman he imitated the style of Antonio Canale but his sheets are dryer. The sureness in the pattern of lines, which the elder Canaletto mastered, was also lacking in Bernardo Bellotto.

34 GIUSEPPE ZAIS: Cavalry Battle. Budapest, Museum of Fine Arts

Morassi also states that, although Zais' drawings do not imitate Zuccarelli's, they frequently bear the apocryphal inscription "Zuccarelli." Thus, in the above-mentioned drawing in Vienna, Zuccarelli's name is inscribed twice, although the signature "Zais P." is distinctly visible on the bridge in the middle.

FRANCESCO GUARDI
School of Venice

Born in Venice in 1712, died there in 1793. He was a pupil and a collaborator of his brother Giovanni Antonio Guardi who was fifteen years his senior, and who has been increasingly appreciated lately by art researchers. Maffei, Bazzani, the two Riccis, Pellegrini and particularly Antonio Canale and Magnasco played important roles in Francesco Guardi's art. In contrast to the majority of the painters of his time, he scarcely ever left the City of the Lagoons. At the most he visited the village of Mastellina in the Val di Sole, in Trento, where his family lived, and he probably visited Rome once. His *vedute*, glimmering with light, and his dazzling pictures of the pageants of Venice made him one of the most outstanding painters of the eighteenth century. His soaring style, his abundance of movement, light and atmosphere make him appear as an early forerunner of the French impressionists. He also painted compositions with figures, although in the case of a great number of these recent research increasingly tends to presume that they were the works of his brother Giannantonio.

As a draughtsman, too, he was outstanding. The same effects as have been pointed to with respect to his paintings appear in his exceedingly witty sketches.

THE CAMPO SS. GIOVANNI E PAOLO IN VENICE. STUDY FOR THE PAINTING OF THE SAME SUBJECT IN THE LOUVRE

PLATE 131

350×581 mm. (13¾″×22⁷/₈″). Pen, wash. From the Esterházy collection. Inv. No. 2814.

Literature

Schönbrunner—Meder, Albertina Publication, No. 686; *S. Meller, 1911*, Cat. No. 160; Szlava Ticharich, *A velencei barocchetto festészete* [The Painting of the Venetian 'Barocchetto']. Budapest, 1929, p. 89 and Plate 7; J. Byam Shaw, *The Drawings of Francesco Guardi.* London, 1949, Fig. 14; V. Moschini, *Guardi.* Milan, 1952, Figs. 67 and 68; L. Vayer, *Master Drawings.* Budapest, 1957, No. 95; *Velencei... rajzok, 1960*, Cat. No. 102, Fig. 21.

In the publication of the Albertina it was presented as Canaletto's work (No. 686), and Simon Meller displayed it under the same name at the Exhibition of the Department of Prints and Drawings in 1911 (No. 160). Szlava Ticharich attributed the drawing to Francesco Guardi and published it as a study to this artist's painting at the Louvre. The drawing is a telling example of the fact that Guardi, this supreme master of *vedute* and *capricci*, notwithstanding his overbrimming fantasy, drew accurately and in accordance with reality when he considered this necessary in preparing a preliminary study to a painting. The drawing corresponds faithfully with the painting.

GIOVANNI BATTISTA CASANOVA
School of Venice

Born in Venice in 1730, died in Dresden in 1795. He was the younger brother of Francesco and of Giacomo Casanova. According to tradition he was a pupil of Piazzetta's but fairly soon left for Rome with Raphael Mengs and worked there for ten years as his pupil and assistant. He became completely subject to the neo-classicist influence of the German master. Like his two brothers, he, too, travelled about Europe a great deal. Winckelmann, for whom he made drawings of antique monuments, called him "the best draughtsman in Rome."

GIOVANNI BATTISTA PIRANESI

Schools of Venice and Rome

Born at Mogliano (Mestre) in 1720, died in Rome in 1778. In Venice he worked at the Valeriani brothers' studio of stage decoration. He learned perspective from Carlo Zucchi and architecture from his uncle Matteo Lucchesi. In 1740 he went to Rome as the draughtsman of the Venetian Legation. His fondness for Palladio's art reveals that he was destined to rediscover antique Rome. In 1743 he returned to Venice, where he is said to have worked for a time at Giambattista Tiepolo's workshop. Then, back in Rome, he commenced his large-scale activity as an etcher. Ancient Rome—*Roma Antica*—was his eternal theme. His art was rooted in that of Michele Marieschi and Marco Ricci who had already produced etchings on the same subject. Two tendencies are predominant in his art. One testifies to the free flight of his fantasy, as in the series of etchings called '*Carceri.*' The other is a persistent adherence to reality. For the latter his *veduti* of Rome offer very good examples. As a drawer of figures he has become particularly appreciate in recent decades.

PLATE 135 MAN RECLINING ON A SOFA

Verso: Sketches in pencil

195×265 mm. (7⅝″×10⅜″). Pen, bistre. Acquired in 1960. Inv. No. 60.1 K.

Literature

I. Fenyő, Dessins italiens inconnus du XVe au XVIIIe siècle. *Bulletin du Musée National Hongrois des Beaux-Arts*, No. 22, 1963, pp. 89—123.

The drawing was identified by the author as Piranesi's work. The capricious and witty interplay of lines and the manner of shading—which forms the shapes by a few parallel lines only—convincingly speak for Piranesi as the artist. The Rococo lightness and Venetian gracefulness of the sketches of hands, drawn with veritable virtuosity on the edge of the sheet, also point to Piranesi. The grotesque realism of its delineation and the freedom and boldness of its fleeting sketchiness set this exceedingly witty Budapest sheet which has emerged but recently among the most important drawings with figures in the master's *oeuvre.* (Cf. Thomas Hylton, *The Drawings of Giovanni Battista Piranesi.* London, without date.)

Closest to our drawing is a sketch at the Ashmolean Museum at Oxford, entitled "Young Man." (H. Thomas, *The Drawings of Giovanni Battista Piranesi.* London, undated. Fig. 68.) Compare the Budapest drawing also to a sheet of the Skippe Collection. (*The Skippe Collection of Old Master Drawings.* Christie's Catalogue. London, November, 1958. Introduction by A.E. Popham. Lot. 157. Plate 27.)

Pietro Antonio Novelli

Born in Venice in 1729, died there in 1804. He was a painter, etcher and writer. In his paintings the effect of Jacopo Amigoni and subsequently that of Piazzetta made itself felt. He stayed in Bologna (1773) and several times in Rome (1779), and became acquainted with the art of Reni and the Carraccis as well as with the neo-classicism of Pompeo Batoni and Anton Raphael Mengs. Only few altarpieces by his hand are known. He produced frescoes at Padua, Carnia and Friaul. As a draughtsman he is characterized by Rococo gracefulness, but also by a certain superficiality. Piazzetta's influence is particularly marked in his drawings, in fact they often look like imitations of this master's sheets, whereas his etchings show the effect Rembrandt had on him. He was among the most prolific illustrators of his time (Tasso, Goldoni, Metastasio, etc.).

PORTRAIT OF AN ARTIST

PLATE 136

238×201 mm. (9⅜″×7⅞″). Pen and wash. Presented by Ignác Gond. Inv. No. 1912-763.

Literature

Velencei... rajzok, 1960, Cat. No. 93.

Edith Hoffmann attributed the drawing to Novelli and pointed out in her handwritten catalogue the relationship between this drawing and a sheet of the master's at the Albertina. (*Albertina, I, 1926*, No. 403.) In "*Arte Veneta*" there appeared a reproduction of a charming drawing, the "Portrait of a Watch-maker" from the Cooper Union Museum in New York, which seems to be akin to Novelli's drawings in Budapest, particularly to the "Portrait of an Artist." (W.R. Rearick, Italian Eighteenth-Century Drawings at Wellesley College. *Arte Veneta*, XIII—XIV, 1959—1960, p. 293, Fig. 365.)

Pietro Antonio Novelli

THE CARD-PLAYER

PLATE 137

250×200 mm. (9⅞″×7⅞″). Pen. From the Delhaes collection. Inv. No. 2702.

Literature

Velencei... rajzok, 1960, Cat. No. 97.

The attribution of this sheet, too, is due to Edith Hoffmann. Its analogies can be found at the Albertina in Vienna, and in the Collection of Drawings at

LORENZO SACCHETTI

PLATE 143 A PALACE IN A PARK. DESIGN FOR A STAGE SET

In the foreground, trees cut out of paper and subsequently pasted on. Page of a sketch-book with designs for stage sets.
The dimensions of the sketch-book are 292×197 mm. (11½″×7¾″). From the Delhaes collection. Inv. No. 2711.

Literature
M. Aggházy, 1950, pp. 69—76; *Velencei... rajzok, 1960*, Cat. No. 109, Fig. 22.

The Department of Prints and Drawings of the Museum of Fine Arts in Budapest has a rich collection of Sacchetti's works, among them two sketch-books. This charming study radiating the playful spirit of the Rococo is, along with a great number of similar drawings, in one of the sketch-books in Budapest. The cover is inscribed: "No. 6. 1793 Lorenzo Sacchetti." The first page of the book reads: "*Libro di Abozzi p le Scene nel Teatro di S: M: R: Imp:*[re] *in Vienna, principiato il Giorno 14 Luglio 1794 giorno dell'arrivo mio in Vienna alle ore 3 della matina vigilia di S: Anna*" (and the name "Giacomo" is crossed out).

It should also be mentioned that above the confusedly and rapidly drawn sketches of scenic architecture on the first page of the sketch-book, there is the following entry: "*Schizzo segnato da Salvatore Vigano 1784-.*" This means that in the year when his master, Domenico Fossati, died (1784), Sacchetti was working together with Salvatore Vigano who was a choreographer and later became *primo ballerino* and then *maestro di ballo* at the Hoftheater in Vienna. (Aggházy, 1950, p. 73 and Note 16.)

LORENZO SACCHETTI

PLATE 144 ANTIQUE RUINS. DESIGN FOR A STAGE SET

Verso: Various sketches in red chalk
398×252 mm. (15⅝″×10⅛″). Pen, brush, blue wash, body-white. *Provenance* unknown. Inv. No. 58.264 K.

Literature
I. Fenyő, 1958, p. 68, Fig. 46; *Velencei ... rajzok, 1960*, Cat. No. 114.

The author selected this fine sheet—almost worthy of a master like Francesco Guardi—in 1957, along with several other drawings in the heap of hitherto unidentified anonymous works at the Museum, as Sacchetti's works. (*I. Fenyő, 1958*, p. 69.) This attribution is so unequivocal that it hardly needs explanation. No one but Sacchetti could draw stage sets of classicist taste with such an authentic Rococo atmosphere. This is certainly an early work of the master's, for he later increasingly developed towards pure classicism. In the pictorial Rococo quality of the representation, Sacchetti is still close to his master, Domenico Fossati (1743—1784) whose designs for stage were characterized by harmony of the lightness of picturesque wash and strokes of the pen.

ADDENDA AND CORRIGENDA

When the printing of the book was almost completed, Philip Pouncey visited our Museum. He pointed out a few errors, made some time before, in the attribution of the drawings published here.

Plate No. 9. The drawing is by Baccio Bandinelli.
Plate No. 11. The drawing is by Biagio Pupini (dalle Lame).
Plate No. 83. Philip Pouncey agrees with Otto Benesch'opinion, who thinks this sheet to be closer to the art of Lodovico Carracci than to that of the Strozzis.
Plate No. 84. The drawing is the work of the so-called "Pseudo Castello."
Plate No. 89. Pouncey is of the opinion that this sheet is a copy. In spite of the undeniable weaknesses of the drawing the author does not agree with this view.

PLATES

1 Anonymous, Lombardy or Bologna, beginning of the fifteenth century: Hunting Adventure

8 Anonymous, Venice, about 1500: Recumbent Woman, Mary (?)

9 BERNARDINO LUINI: Seated Woman

10 Bartolomeo Montagna: The Madonna and Child

11 GAUDENZIO FERRARI: The Four Evangelists

12 GIORGIONE: St. Elizabeth with the Infant St. John

13 Girolamo Romanino: The Nativity

22 Domenico Campagnola: David and Goliath

23 Follower of Domenico Campagnola: Mountainous Landscape with Antique Ruins

26 Camillo Boccaccino: A Holy Bishop

27 Unknown follower of Giorgione, about 1530: Dancing Figures in Landscape

32 PARMIGIANINO: Proserpina Changing Ascalaphus into an Owl

33 PARMIGIANINO: Two models

40 LUCA CAMBIASO: The Holy Family in Front of a House

41 Luca Cambiaso: Madonna and Child with the Infant St. John and St. Catherine

42 LUCA CAMBIASO: The Three Theological Virtues

43 Luca Cambiaso: The Last Judgement

44 Bernardo Castello: Battle Scene

45 BERNARDO CASTELLO: Scene in a Camp

46 JACOPO TINTORETTO: Study after the so-called 'Atlas'

47 Verso of Plate 46: A variant of the same subject

48 JACOPO TINTORETTO: Two studies after the so-called 'Atlas'

49. Verso of Plate 48: Study after the same figure

50 Jacopo Tintoretto or his workshop: Man Bending, Seen from the Back

51 Jacopo Tintoretto, workshop: The Emperor Vitellius

54 Paolo Veronese: Peter of Amiens before the Doge Vitale Michiel

55 Verso of Plate 54: A traced variant of the same scene

56 PAOLO VERONESE: The Execution of a Martyr (?) and other sketches

57 PAOLO VERONESE: Christ in the House of Simon

60 PALMA IL GIOVANE: The Brazen Serpent

61 Palma il Giovane: A Naval Battle between Turks and Venetians

62a Verso of Plate 60: The Gathering of Manna

62b Verso of Plate 61: The Gathering of Manna

63 PALMA IL GIOVANE: St. Jerome

64 PALMA IL GIOVANE:
Pietà and Head of a Bearded Man.
Verso of the following Plate

65a PALMA IL GIOVANE:
The Miracle of the Loaves and Fishes.
Recto of the preceding Plate

65b PALMA IL GIOVANE:
The Miracle of the Loaves and Fishes.
Painting in the Church of the Carmini in Venice

66 PALMA IL GIOVANE: Adoration of the Magi

67 ANONYMOUS, VENICE, END OF THE SIXTEENTH CENTURY (ANDREA VICENTINO ?): The Judgement of Paris

68 ANONYMOUS, VENICE, ABOUT 1600: The Funeral of a Saint

69 GIOVANNI BATTISTA TROTTI (MALOSSO):
St. Homobonus and St. Himerius
Commend the Town of Cremona to the Patronage of the Madonna

74 GIULIO CESARE PROCACCINI: Sketches to a "St. Andrew"

75 Verso of Plate 74: Sketches to a composition of "The Last Supper"

76 Pier Francesco Morazzone (P.F. Mazuchelli): St. Francis before the Sultan

77 PIER FRANCESCO MORAZZONE (P.F. MAZUCHELLI): The Fire-Ordeal of St. Francis before the Sultan

78 GIOVANNI BATTISTA MAURO DELLA ROVERE (IL FIAMMENGHINO): Moses; above him a Putto with a Book and a Serpent

79 Giovanni Battista Mauro della Rovere: Christ Appearing before his **Disciples**

80 Marcantonio Bassetti: Moses Striking Water from the Rock

81 Domenico Fetti (?): Woman Reading

82 SEBASTIANO MAZZONI (?): Young Amor Chastised by Nymphs

83 BERNARDO STROZZI: Christ and the Woman of Samaria

86 GIULIO CARPIONI: Clearing in a Forest with a Sleeping Man

87 GIULIO CARPIONI: A sheet of sketches with bacchantes, a river-god, the Magdalene (?) and other figures

88 ANTONIO ZANCHI (?): Alexander the Great before the Body of Darius

89 PIETRO LIBERI: The Death of Adonis

90 ANONYMOUS, NORTHERN ITALY (MILAN?), BEGINNING OF THE SEVENTEENTH CENTURY: Head of a Monk

91 Anonymous. Northern Italy (Milan?), beginning of the seventeenth century:
Head of a Bishop

92 GIOVANNI BENEDETTO CASTIGLIONE: Allegory in Honour of the Duchess of Mantua

93 GIOVANNI BENEDETTO CASTIGLIONE: The Assumption of the Virgin

94 GIOVANNI BENEDETTO CASTIGLIONE: A sheet of sketches

95 GIOVANNI BENEDETTO CASTIGLIONE: Fauns Fighting

98 ANONYMOUS, VENICE, BEGINNING OF THE EIGHTEENTH CENTURY (ANDREA CELESTI?): Esther before Ahasuerus

99 Sebastiano Ricci: Hercules at the Cross-roads

102 GIOVANNI BATTISTA PITTONI: A detail of the composition "The Glorification of Newton"

103 GIOVANNI BATTISTA PITTONI: The Nativity

104 GIOVANNI BATTISTA PITTONI: The Adoration of the Magi

105 Gaspare Diziani: The Madonna with St. Nicholas, St. Sebastian and a Third Saint in a Rococo Frame

106 GASPARE DIZIANI: St. Anthony Kneeling before the Madonna

107 GASPARE DIZIANI: The Nativity

108 Gaspare Diziani: The Magdalene

109 GASPARE DIZIANI: Fighting Knights

110 GASPARE DIZIANI: Aeneas and Anchises

111 GASPARE DIZIANI: The Raising of the Youth of Nain

112 GASPARE DIZIANI: Boreas, the God of Winds Abducting Oreithyia

113 GASPARE DIZIANI: The Rape of Helen

114 Gaspare Diziani (?): Minerva Enthroned on Clouds

115 Verso of Plate 114: A similar representation

116a Gaspare Diziani (?):
The Madonna Appearing to St. Francis

116b Gaspare Diziani (?):
Design for a monument with the figure of Fame

7 GASPARE DIZIANI (?): Merchants before the Doge. (Sketch to a ceiling)

118 Giovanni Battista Tiepolo: Study of a figure for the fresco on the ceiling of the staircase in the Archbishop's residence at Würzburg

119 Verso of Plate 118: A Study of the Madonna

120 GIOVANNI BATTISTA TIEPOLO: Study

121 Giovanni Battista Tiepolo: A study for the figure of Thetis

122 GIOVANNI DOMENICO TIEPOLO: Study of a head after Giovanni Battista Tiepolo's painting in the Museum of Fine Arts in Budapest: "St. James of Compostella on Horseback"

123 GIOVANNI DOMENICO TIEPOLO: The Assumption of the Virgin

124a FRANCESCO FONTEBASSO:
A sheet of studies with the head
of a woman and two putti

124b FRANCESCO FONTEBASSO:
A sheet of studies with the head
of a bearded man and two hands

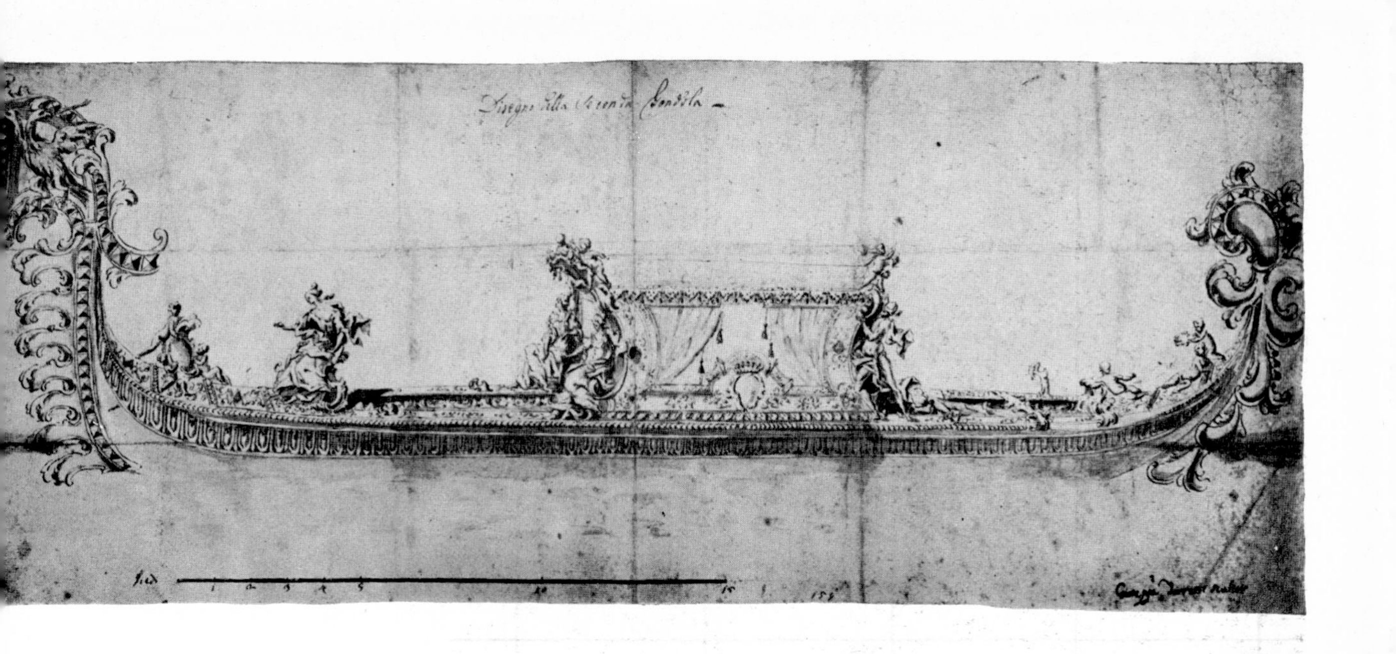

125 GIUSEPPE BERNARDI (TORRETTI): The Second Gondola

126 GIUSEPPE BAZZANI: The Presentation at the Temple

127 Verso of Plate 126: Four studies of heads

128 MARCO RICCI: Landscape

129 Bernardo Bellotto (Canaletto): The Porta Pontecorvo and the Church of Sta Giustina at Padua as Seen from the Bastioni

130 GIUSEPPE ZAIS: Landscape with a River and a Stone Bridge

131 FRANCESCO GUARDI: The Campo SS. Giovanni e Paolo in Venice.
Study for the painting of the same subject in the Louvre

132 GIOVANNI BATTISTA CASANOVA: Design for a group

133: FRANCESCO CASANOVA: Study of a Rider

134a, b ANTONIO MARIA DI GIROLAMO ZANETTI: The Madonna and Child

135 Giovanni Battista Piranesi: Man Reclining on a Sofa

136 PIETRO ANTONIO NOVELLI: Portrait of an Artist

137 PIETRO ANTONIO NOVELLI: The Card-Player

138 Pietro Antonio Novelli: St. Lawrence and an Angel Commend a Venetian Patrician to the Madonna's Protection. Design for an altar-piece

139 FRANCESCO ZUGNO: Minerva in the Library

142 LORENZO SACCHETTI: A Colonnade in Moonlight. Design for a stage set

143 Lorenzo Sacchetti: A Palace in a Park. Design for a stage set

144 LORENZO SACCHETTI: Antique Ruins. Design for a stage set

APPENDIX

LIST OF DRAWINGS CONNECTED WITH PAINTINGS AND PRINTS

FRANCESCO BONSIGNORI (?): The Madonna and Child. The drawing greatly corresponds with Liberale da Verona's painting in the National Gallery in London, Fig. 4. — PLATE 5

FRANCESCO BONSIGNORI (?): St. Christopher. *Verso* of Plate 5. The figure of the Saint corresponds with that of St. Christopher in the altarpiece of S. Fermo Maggiore, Verona, Museo di Castelvecchio, Fig. 3. — FIG. 2

GIROLAMO ROMANINO: The Nativity. Preparatory drawing to Romanino's painting at Brescia, Pinacoteca Tosio e Martinengo, Fig. 11. — PLATE 13

CORREGGIO: Madonna Enthroned in Clouds. Sketch to the *Tribuna* fresco of "The Coronation of the Virgin" in the Church of S. Giovanni Evangelista at Parma. Preserved today in fragment at the Pinacoteca of Parma. In the eighteenth century C.M. Metz made an engraving after the drawing. The fragment is reproduced by G. Gronau, Correggio. *Klass. d. Kunst.* Stuttgart, 1907, Fig. 54. — PLATE 16

CORREGGIO: Christ Enthroned in Clouds. Sketch to the *Tribuna* fresco of "The Coronation of the Virgin" in the Church of S. Giovanni Evangelista at Parma. Preserved today in fragment in the Pinacoteca of Parma. Reproduced by G. Gronau, Correggio. *Klass. d. Kunst.* Stuttgart, 1907. Fig. 54. — PLATE 17 and FIG. 12

CORREGGIO: Composition with Two Female Figures. In the seventeenth century Hendrick van der Borcht made an engraving after this drawing. — PLATE 18

CAMILLO BOCCACCINO: A Holy Bishop. Sketch to Camillo Boccaccino's altarpiece "Madonna with Saints" at the Narodní Galerie in Prague, dated 1525, Fig. 13. Preparatory drawing to the figure of the bishop in the left-hand side of the painting. — PLATE 26

PARMIGIANINO: St. Cecilia, on the *verso*, Plate 28: Two studies of a David figure. Studies to paintings on the organ wings in the Church of Sta. Maria della Steccata at Parma. A further sketch to the figure of St. Cecilia is in the Louvre, in Paris (Inv. No. 6456). — PLATE 29

PARMIGIANINO: Two Female Nudes. *Verso* of Plate 30. Sketches to the virgins in the Church of Sta. Maria della Steccata at Parma. — PLATE 31

PARMIGIANINO: Proserpina Changing Ascalaphus into an Owl. An engraving after this composition by Parmigianino was made by Enea Vico. (Bartsch, XV, p. 303. No. 45.) Further designs to Proserpina's figure are in the British Museum (Inv. No. Ff. 1—79) and on the sheet "Lucretia" by Parmigianino in Budapest (Inv. No. 1531). — PLATE 32

PAOLO VERONESE: Peter of Amiens before the Doge Vitale Michiel. Sketches to a painting of Veronese's at the M. Istituto d'Arte 'A. Passaglia' at Lucca. The artist made the painting as a model for a carpet in the Sala del Collegio. Published by R. Pallucchini, *Mostra di Paolo Veronese.* Venice, 1939, No. 73. Engraved by Antonio Lorenzini in the beginning of the eighteenth century. Published by *E. Hoffmann, 1927*, p. 139, Fig. 25. — PLATES 54 and 55

PALMA IL GIOVANE: The Miracle of the Loaves and Fishes. Preparatory drawing to Palma's painting in the Church of del Carmine in Venice, Plate 65b. — PLATE 65a

MALOSSO: St. Homobonus and St. Himerius Commend the Town of Cremona to the Patronage of the Madonna. The drawing is a preparatory sketch to the group in the left-hand side of Malosso's painting at the Pinacoteca at Cremona, Fig. 16. — PLATE 69

PLATE 71 MONCALVO: The Birth of the Virgin. Preparatory drawing to the painting of Moncalvo at the Museo Civico at Pavia, Fig. 17.

PLATE 76 MORAZZONE: St. Francis before the Sultan. Presumably a preparatory drawing to the fresco in the second cloister of the Church of Sant'Angelo in Milan.

PLATE 77 MORAZZONE: The Fire-Ordeal of St. Francis before the Sultan. The drawing corresponds with the engraving by Girolamo Ferroni, made in 1723 after Morazzone's fresco in the second cloister of Sant'Angelo in Milan (Fig. 19). In the meantime Morazzone's frescoes became ruined.

PLATE 85 JOHANN CARL LOTH: Jupiter and Mercury with Philemon and Baucis. Preparatory drawing to J.C. Loth's painting at the Kunsthistorisches Museum in Vienna, Fig. 20.

PLATE 89 PIETRO LIBERI: The Death of Adonis. Preparatory drawing to Liberi's painting at the Palazzo Conti at Padua, Fig. 21.

PLATE 92 G.B. CASTIGLIONE: Allegory in Honour of the Duchess of Mantua. The drawing as well as three sheets in the Windsor collection are closely connected with a painting of Castiglione, which was formerly in the Collection Pellicioli. Published by G. Delogu, Pittori Genovesi del '600. *L'Arte*, 1929, p. 175.

PLATE 96 G.A. ANSALDO: Allegory of Ferdinand Medici II. Design to a painting by Ansaldo (Ligozzi?) in the Pitti Gallery in Florence, published by E. Hoffmann. 1942, Fig. 25.

PLATE 102 G.B. PITTONI: A detail of the composition "The Glorification of Newton." The sheet is a faithful replica of the group in the centre of Pittoni's painting at the Marzotto Collection at Valdagno and of another painting by him, which is in a private collection in Rome, published by *I. Fenyő*, *1959*, Figs. 49, 50.

PLATE 103 G.B. PITTONI: The Nativity. The drawing is closely connected with numerous "*Presepio*"-paintings of Pittoni, first of all with the pictures at Cordenons and at the Pinakothek in Munich. The painting at Cordenons was published by Laura Coggiola-Pittoni, *G.B. Pittoni*. Florence, 1921, Fig. 2; the picture in Munich by C. Donzelli, *I pittori veneti del Settecento*. Florence, 1957, Fig. 271.

PLATE 104 G.B. PITTONI: The Adoration of the Magi. The drawing tallies in full with Pittoni's altarpiece in the Church of Mary in Cracow, published by J. Białostocki and M. Waliczki *Europäische Malerei in polnischen Sammlungen*, Fig. 376.

PLATE 118 G.B. TIEPOLO: Study of a figure for the fresco on the ceiling of the staircase in the Archbishop's residence at Würzburg, published by A. Morassi, *G.B. Tiepolo. His Life and Work*. London, 1955, Plate 62.

PLATE 121 G.B. TIEPOLO: A study for the figure of Thetis. Study to the mural painting entitled "The Glorification of Spain" Tiepolo painted for the throne-room of the Royal Palace in Madrid, published by A. Morassi, *G. B. Tiepolo. His Life and Work*. London, 1955, Fig. 87.

PLATE 122 G.D. TIEPOLO: Study of a head after Giovanni Battista Tiepolo's painting in the Museum of Fine Arts in Budapest: "St. James of Compostella on Horseback," published by A. Morassi, *G.B. Tiepolo. His Life and Work*. London, 1955, Fig. 64.

PLATE 129 BERNARDO BELLOTTO: The Porta Pontecorvo and the Church of Sta. Giustina at Padua as Seen from the Bastioni. Free copy after the drawing of Antonio Canale at Windsor, published by K.T. Parker, *The Drawings of Antonio Canaletto... at Windsor Castle*. Oxford, London, 1948, Fig. 55. Bellotto used the Budapest sheet as a preparatory drawing for an etching. A. De Vesme, *Le peintre-graveur italien*, 1906, p. 490, No. 2.

PLATE 131 FRANCESCO GUARDI: The Campo SS. Giovanni e Paolo in Venice. Preparatory drawing to a painting by Guardi in the Louvre, published by V. Moschini, *Guardi*. Milan, 1952, Fig. 68.

PLATES 134a and 134b ANTONIO MARIA DI GIROLAMO ZANETTI: The Madonna and Child. Both are drawings for *clair-obscur* woodcuts Zanetti made after Parmigianino. (Bartsch, 5.)

BIBLIOGRAPHY

M. Aggházy, 1950 = Aggházy, M., Scenografie di Lorenzo Sacchetti. *La Critica d'Arte*, III. serie, anno IX, No. 1, May, 1950.

Albertina, I, 1926 = *Beschreibender Katalog der Handzeichnungen in der Graphischen Sammlung Albertina*, Vol. I. *Die Zeichnungen der Venezianischen Schule.* Bearbeitet von Alfred Stix und L. Fröhlich-Bum. Vienna, 1926.

Albertina, III, 1932 — *Beschreibender Katalog der Handzeichnungen in der Graphischen Sammlung Albertina*, Vol. III. *Die Zeichnungen der Toskanischen, Umbrischen und Römischen Schulen.* Bearbeitet von Alfred Stix und L. Fröhlich-Bum.

Albertina, VI, 1941 = *Beschreibender Katalog der Handzeichnungen in der Graphischen Sammlung Albertina*, Vol. VI. *Die Schulen von Ferrara, Bologna, Parma und Modena, der Lombardei, Genuas, Neapels und Siziliens, mit einem Nachtrag zu allen italienischen Schulen.* Bearbeitet von A. Stix und A. Spitzmüller. Vienna, 1941.

Algarotti, F., *Lettere sulla pittura.* Venice, 1792.

Armenino, G. B., *De' veri precetti della pittura.* Ravenna, 1587.

Arslan, E., Alcuni dipinti per il McSwiny. *Rivista d'Arte*, XIV, 1932, pp. 128—140.

Arslan, E., *Inventario degli oggetti d'arte d'Italia*, VII. *Provincia di Padova.* Rome, 1936.

Arslan, E., Cinque disegni veneti. *Arte Veneta*, VIII, 1954, pp. 289—294.

Arslan, E., *Catalogo delle cose d'arte e di antichità d'Italia. Vicenza I. Le chiese.* Rome, 1956.

Arslan, E., *Contributo a Sebastiano Ricci e ad Antonio Francesco Peruzzini.* Off-print from *Studies in the History of Art.* Dedicated to William E. Suida on his eightieth birthday. 1959.

Arslan, E., *Le pitture del Duomo di Milano.* Milan, 1960.

Baldinucci, F., *Notizie de' Professori del disegno.* Florence, 1681.

Barelli, E. S., *Disegni di maestri lombardi del primo seicento.* Exhibition catalogue of the Ambrosiana Collection. Milan, 1959.

Bartoli, F., *Notizie delle pitture... delle più rinomate città d'Italia.* Venice, 1776.

Bartsch, A., *Le Peintre-Graveur.* Vienna, 1802—1821.

Bassi, E., Due quadri di Sebastiano Ricci dimenticati. *Arte Veneta*, III, 1949, pp. 121—123.

Bassi-Rathgeb, R., Alcune opere inedite del Fontebasso. *Arte Veneta*, XIII—XIV, 1959—1960, p. 223.

Bassi-Rathgeb, R., Novità documentarie sui pittori Zais. *Arte Veneta*, XIII—XIV, 1959—1960, pp. 242—243.

Bean, J., Les dessins italiens de la collection Bonnat. Bayonne, Musée Bonnat. *Inventaire général des dessins des musées de province.* Paris, 1960.

Benesch, O., Seicentostudien. *Jahrbuch der Kunsthistorischen Sammlungen.* Neue Folge, Vol. I, 1926, pp. 245—268.

Benesch, O., Zu Veronese und Tintoretto. *Belvedere*, VIII, 1929, II, pp. 330—334.

Benesch, O., Meisterzeichungen aus dem oberitalienischen Kunstkreis. *Die Graphischen Künste.* Neue Folge, Vol. I, 1936, pp. 11—20 and 60—66.

Benesch, O., *Venetian Drawings of the Eighteenth Century in America.* New York, 1947.

Benesch, O., Marginalien zur Tiepolo-Ausstellung in Venedig. *Alte und Neue Kunst*, I, 1952.

Benesch, O., *The Drawings of Rembrandt*, Vols. I—VI. London, 1955—1957.

Benesch, O., Tiepolo und die malerische Aufgabe des Freskos im Settecento. *Münchner Jahrbuch der Bildenden Kunst.* Dritte Folge, Vol. VIII, 1957, pp. 211—232.

Benesch, O., con l'assistenza di Konrad Oberhuber, *Disegni veneti dell'Albertina di Vienna.* Exhibition Catalogue. Venice, 1961.

Bercken, E. van der, *Die Gemälde des Jacopo Tintoretto.* Munich, 1942.

Berenson, B., *Lorenzo Lotto.* London, 1956.

Berenson, B., *Italian Pictures of the Renaissance. A List of the Principal Artists and their Works with an Index of Places. Venetian School*, Vols. I—II. London, 1957.

A. Bertini, 1958 = Bertini, A., *I disegni italiani della Biblioteca Reale di Torino.* Rome, 1958.

Bertoletti, A., *Artisti veneti in Roma nei secoli XV, XVI, XVII. Studi e ricerche negli Archivi Romani.* Venice, 1884.

Bettagno, A., *Disegni e dipinti di Giovanni Antonio Pellegrini.* Exhibition Catalogue. Venice, 1959.

Bettagno, A., *Disegni veneti del Settecento della Fondazione Cini e delle Collezioni venete.* Exhibition Catalogue. Venice, 1963.

Białostocki, J. and M. Walicki, *Europäische Malerei in polnischen Sammlungen.* Warsaw, 1957.

Blunt, A., *The Drawings of G.B. Castiglione and Stefano della Bella at Windsor Castle.* London, 1954.

Blunt, A., Drawings by Sebastiano Ricci in the Royal Library. Venezia e Europa. *Atti del XVIII. Congresso Internazionale di Storia dell'Arte.* Venice, 1955, p. 349.

Blunt—Croft-Murray, 1957 = Blunt, A. and E. Croft-Murray: *Venetian Drawings of the XVIIth and XVIIIth Centuries at Windsor Castle.* London, 1957.

Boccassini, G., Profilo dell'Aliense. *Arte Veneta*, XII, 1958. pp. 111—125.

Boschini, M., *La carta del navegar pitoresco.* Venice, 1660.

Boschini, M., *Le ricche minere della pittura veneziana.* Venice, 1674.

Boschini, M., *I gioielli pittoreschi, etc.* Venice, 1676.

Bottari, G. e S. Ticcozzi, *Raccolta di lettere sulla pittura, scultura ed architettura.* Milan, 1822—1825.

Brenzoni, R., *Liberale da Verona.* Milan, 1930.

Briganti, G., *Il Manierismo e Pellegrino Tibaldi.* Rome, 1945.

Brizio, A.M., Note per una definizione critica dello stile di Paolo Veronese. *L'Arte*, XXIX, 1926, pp. 213—243, and XXXI, 1928, pp. 1—10.

Brizio, A.M., *Vercelli, catalogo delle cose d'arte e di antichità d'Italia*, Vol. VIII. Rome, 1935.

Budde, I., *Beschreibender Katalog der Handzeichnungen in der Staatlichen Kunstakademie Düsseldorf.* Düsseldorf, 1930.

Byam Shaw, J., Giovanni Battista Piranesi. *Old Master Drawings*, No. 8, March, 1928, pp. 56—57.

Byam Shaw, J., Liberale da Verona. *Old Master Drawings*, September, 1931, p. 28, Plate 21.

Byam Shaw, J., Some Venetian Draughtsmen of the Eighteenth Century. *Old Master Drawings*, VII, 1932—1933, pp. 47—63.

Byam Shaw, J., *The Drawings of Francesco Guardi.* London, 1949.

Byam Shaw, J., The Drawings of Francesco Fontebasso. *Arte Veneta*, VIII, 1954, pp. 317—325.

Byam Shaw, J., *The Drawings of Domenico Tiepolo.* London, 1962.

Calabi, A., *L'incisione italiana.* Milan, 1931.

Campori, G., *Raccolta di cataloghi ed inventari inediti di quadri, statue, etc.* Modena, 1870.

Chatelet, A., Alcuni disegni veneti del Cinquecento al Museo del Louvre. *Arte Veneta*, VII, 1953, pp. 89—92.

Chatelet, A., Les dessins et gravures de paysage de Domenico Campagnola. Venezia e l'Europa. *Atti del XVIII. Congresso Internazionale di Storia dell'Arte.* Venice, 1956, pp. 258—259.

Chatelet, A., Venetian Drawings from the János Scholz Collection at the Cini Foundation. *The Art Quarterly*, XXI, 1958, pp. 187—199.
Ciampi, M., I disegni di Palma il Giovane esposti a Firenze. *Arte Veneta*, XII, 1958, pp. 251—254.
Cicogna, E., *Delle iscrizioni veneziane.* Venice, 1824—1853.
Coggiola-Pittoni, L., *Dei Pittoni artisti veneti.* Bergamo, 1907.
Coggiola-Pittoni, L., G.B. Pittoni. *Piccola Collezione d'Arte*, No. 26. Florence, 1921.
Coggiola-Pittoni, L., Opere inedite di Giambattista Pittoni. *Dedalo*, 1927—1928, Vol. III, pp. 671—695.
Coggiola-Pittoni, L., *Altre opere inedite di Giambattista Pittoni.* Venice, 1933. Off-print from the *Gazzetta Illustrata.*
Coggiola-Pittoni, L., *Disegni inediti di Giovanni Battista Pittoni.* Off-print from the July Number of the 1934 Volume of *Rivista della Città di Venezia.*
Coletti, L., Treviso. *Catalogo delle cose d'arte e di antichità d'Italia*, Vol. VII. Rome, 1935.
Coletti, L., *Cima da Conegliano.* Venice, 1959.
Constable, W. G., *Canaletto* I—II. Oxford, 1962.
Copertini, G., *Il Parmigianino*, Vols. I—II. Parma, 1932.
Czobor, A , Quadri sconosciuti di Sebastiano Ricci. *Acta Historiae Artium Academiae Scientiarum Hungaricae*, Vol. I, 1954, pp. 301—311.
Damerini, G., *I pittori veneziani del '700.* Bologna, 1928.
Degenhart, B., Zur Graphologie der Handzeichnung. *Kunstgeschichtliches Jahrbuch der Bibliotheca Hertziana*, Vol. I. Leipzig, 1937, pp. 225—343.
Degenhart, B., *Italienische Zeichnungen des frühen 15. Jahrhunderts.* Basel, 1949.
Degenhart, B., Di una pubblicazione su Pisanello e di altri fatti. (I) *Arte Veneta*, VII, 1953, pp. 182—185, and (II) *Arte Veneta*, VIII, 1954, pp. 96—118.
Degenhart, B. and Annegrit Schmitt, *Gentile da Fabriano in Rom und die Anfänge des Antikenstudiums.* Off-print from *Münchner Jahrbuch der Bildenden Kunst.* Dritte Folge, Vol. XI, 1960.
Del Croix, F., *Inediti di Marco Ricci. Commentari*, 1957.
Delogu, G., Di alcuni dipinti inediti dello Strozzi. *L'Arte*, XXXII, 1929, pp. 27—32.
Delogu, G., *Pittori veneti minori del Settecento.* Venice, 1930.
Delogu, G., *Pittori minori liguri, lombardi e piemontesi del Seicento e del Settecento.* Venice, 1931.
Delogu, G., *La pittura italiana del Seicento.* Florence, 1939.
Delogu, G., *Disegni veneziani del Settecento.* Milan and Zurich, 1947.
Delogu, G., *Pittura veneziana dal XIV. al XVIII. secolo.* Bergamo, 1958.
Derschau, J. von, *Sebastiano Ricci.* Heidelberg, 1922.
De Vesme, A., *Le peintre-graveur italien.* Milan, 1906.
Dobroklonsky, M., Liberale da Verona. *Old Master Drawings*, Vol, IV, June, 1929, pp. 3—4, Plate 9.
Dobroklonsky, M., Государственный Эрмитаж. Рисунки итальянской школы XV и XVI веков. [Ermitage of the State. Drawings of the Italian School of the fifteenth-sixteenth centuries.] Moscow, Leningrad, 1940.
Dobroklonsky, M., Quelques feuilles inédites de Fontebasso aux Musées de Leningrad. *Arte Veneta*, XII, 1958, pp. 186—189.
Dobroklonsky, M., Государственный Эрмитаж. Рисунки итальянской школы XVII–XVIII веков. [Ermitage of the State. Drawings of the Italian School of the fifteenth-sixteenth centuries]. Catalogue. Leningrad, 1961.
Donzelli, C., *I pittori veneti del Settecento.* Florence, 1957.
Dussler, L., *Giovanni Bellini.* Vienna, 1949.
Ewald, G., Loth a Venezia, le pale d'altare. *Critica d'Arte*, 1959, VI, Fasc. 31, pp. 43—51.

Ghidiglia Quintavalle, A., Jacopo Palma il Giovane nel Modenese e nel Reggiano. *Arte Veneta*, XI, 1957, pp. 129—142.

Ghidiglia Quintavalle, A., *Michelangelo Anselmi.* Parma, 1960.

Ghidiglia Quintavalle A. and A. C. Quintavalle, *Arte in Emilia.* Parma, 1960—1961.

Ghidiglia Quintavalle, A., *Arte in Emilia* (seconda). Parma, 1962.

Giglioli, O. H., Mostra di disegni veneti agli Uffizi. *Emporium*, 1936, p. 316.

Gnudi, C., Giunte al Mazzoni. *La Critica d'Arte*, I, 1935—1936, pp. 181—183.

Gombosi, G., Veronese. *Magyar Művészet*, IV, 1928, pp. 721—732.

Gombosi, G., *Moretto da Brescia.* Basel, 1943.

Göring, M., Zur Kritik und Datierung der Werke des Giovanni Battista Pittoni. *Mitteilungen des Kunsthistorischen Institutes in Florenz*, Vol. 4, 1932—1934, pp. 201—248.

Göring, M., Pellegrini-Studien. *Münchner Jahrbuch der Bildenden Kunst.* Neue Folge, 1937, Vol. XII, pp. 233—250.

Göring, M., Paolo Veronese und das Settecento. *Jahrbuch der Preußischen Kunstsammlungen*, LXI, 1940, pp. 100—124.

Grassi, L., Gaudenzio Ferrari e i suoi disegni. *L'Arte.* Nuova serie, Vol. XII, 1941, pp. 182—205.

Grassi, L., *Il disegno italiano dal Trecento al Seicento.* Rome, 1956.

Gregori, M., Traccia per Camillo Boccaccino. *Paragone*, No. 37, 1953, pp. 3—18.

Gregori, M., Altobello, il Romanino e il Cinquecento Cremonese. *Paragone*, VI, No. 69, 1955, pp. 3—28.

Gregori, M., *Il Morazzone.* Exhibition catalogue. Varese, 14th July—14th October. Milan, 1962.

Grossato, L., *Il Museo Civico di Padova*, Venice, 1957.

Grosso, O. and A. Pettorelli, *Genova. I disegni di Palazzo Bianco.* Milan, 1910.

D. v. Hadeln, 1922 = Hadeln, D. von, *Zeichnungen des Giacomo Tintoretto.* Berlin, 1922.

Hadeln, D. v., *Zeichnungen des Tizian.* Berlin, 1924.

Hadeln, D. v., Some Drawings by Tintoretto. *The Burlington Magazine*, XLIV, 1924, pp. 278—284.

D. v. Hadeln, 1925, Quattrocento = Hadeln, D. von, *Venezianische Zeichnungen des Quattrocento.* Berlin, 1925.

D. v. Hadeln, 1925 = Hadeln, D. von, *Zeichnungen der Hochrenaissance.* Berlin, 1925.

D. v. Hadeln, 1926 = Hadeln, D. von, *Venezianische Zeichnungen der Spätrenaissance.* Berlin, 1926.

Hadeln, D.v., *Handzeichnungen von G. B. Tiepolo*, Vols. I—II. Munich, 1927.

D. v. Hadeln, 1930 = Hadeln, D. von, *Die Zeichnungen von Antonio Canale, genannt Canaletto.* Vienna, 1930.

Halm, P., B. Degenhart, W. Wegner, *Hundert Meisterzeichnungen aus der Staatlichen Graphischen Sammlung.* Munich, 1958.

Haskell, F., *Patrons and Painters.* London, 1963.

Haumann, I., *Das oberitalienische Landschaftsbild des Settecento.* Straßburg, 1927.

Heil, W., Palma Giovane als Zeichner. *Jahrbuch der Preußischen Kunstsammlungen*, XLVII, 1926, pp. 58—71.

Heinz, G., Studien zu den Quellen der dekorativen Malerei im venezianischen Settecento. *Arte Veneta*, X, 1956, pp. 142—148.

Hind, A. M., *Early Italian Engraving.* London, 1938—1948, Vols. I—VII.

E. Hoffmann, 1927 = Hoffmann, E., *A Szépművészeti Múzeum néhány olasz rajzáról* [On Some Italian Drawings of the Museum of Fine Arts in Budapest], Az Országos Magyar Szépművészeti Múzeum Évkönyvei [Year-Books of the Hungarian Museum of Fine Arts]. Vol. IV, 1927, pp. 116—173.

E. Hoffmann, 1930 = Hoffmann, E., *Miniatúrák és olasz rajzok* [Miniatures and Italian Drawings]. Exhibition catalogue of the Department of Prints and Drawings of the Museum of Fine Arts in Budapest, 1930.

E. Hoffmann, Magyar Művészet, 1930 = Hoffmann, E., Miniatúrák és olasz rajzok kiállítása a Szépművészeti Múzeumban [Exhibition of Miniatures and Italian Drawings in the Museum of Fine Arts in Budapest). *Magyar Művészet*, VI, 1930, pp. 181—199.

E. Hoffmann, 1931 = Hoffmann, E., Újabb meghatározások a rajzgyűjteményben (Recent Attributions in the Collection of Drawings), pp. 8—46. *Az Országos Magyar Szépművészeti Múzeum Évkönyvei* [Year-Books of the Museum of Fine Arts in Budapest], Vol. VI, 1931, pp. 129—206.

E. Hoffmann, 1941 = Hoffmann, E., Elveszett Dürer-rajzok és néhány olasz rajz a Szépművészeti Múzeumban [Lost Drawings by Dürer and Some Italian Drawings in the Museum of Fine Arts]. *Az Országos Magyar Szépművészeti Múzeum Évkönyvei* [Year-Books of the Museum of Fine Arts in Budapest], Vol. X, 1941, pp. 7—46.

Ivanoff, N., Andrea Celesti e gli albori del '700 veneziano. *Vernice*, 1948, No. 19, p. 4.

Ivanoff, N., Questioni riccesche. *Emporium*, 1948.

Ivanoff, N., Gli affreschi del Liberi e del Celesti nella Villa Rinaldi Barbini di Asolo. *Arte Veneta*, III, 1949, pp. 111—114.

Ivanoff, N., *Mostra del Bazzani. Saggio critico e catalogo delle opere.* Exhibition catalogue. Mantua, 1950.

Ivanoff, N., Appunti su Marco Ricci. *Emporium*, 1950.

Ivanoff, N., Le pitture Settecentesche nella Chiesa dello Spirito Santo. *Arte Veneta*, IX, 1955, pp. 220—222.

Ivanoff, N., Stile e maniera. *Saggi e Memorie di Storia dell'Arte*, I. Venice, 1957, pp. 107—163.

Ivanoff, N., Disegni dei Procaccini. *Critica d'Arte*, V, 1958, pp. 223—232.

Ivanoff, N., Ignoti disegni Lombardi del Sei- e Settecento. *Emporium*, LXV, 1959, pp. 7—14.

Ivanoff, N., *I disegni italiani del Seicento.* Venice, 1959.

Ivanoff, N., Sebastiano Mazzoni. *Saggi e Memorie di Storia dell'Arte*, II. Venice, 1959, pp. 211—279.

Klauner, F., Venezianische Landschaftsdarstellung von Jacopo Bellini bis Tizian. *Jahrbuch der Kunsthistorischen Sammlungen in Wien*, Vol. LIV, 1958, pp. 121—150, Fig. 161.

Knox, G., *Catalogue of the Tiepolo Drawings in the Victoria and Albert Museum.* London, 1960.

Kurz, O., Giorgio Vasari's Libro dei disegni. *Old Master Drawings*, XII, 1937, Nos. 45 and 47.

Kutschera-Woborsky, O., Sebastiano Riccis Arbeiten für Turin. *Monatshefte für Kunstwissenschaft*, VIII, 1915, pp. 397—408.

Lanzi, L., *Storia pittorica della Italia dal Risorgimento delle Belle Arti fin presso al fine del XVIII. secolo.* Bassano, 1789.

Lazareff, V., Beiträge zu Bernardo Strozzi. *Münchner Jahrbuch der Bildenden Kunst.* Neue Folge, VI, 1929, pp. 7—30.

Lavagnino, E., *L'opera del genio italiano all estero: Gli artisti in Germania.* Rome, 1943.

Lavallée, P., *Les techniques du dessin.* Paris, 1943.

Lechi, F., with the collaboration of Gaetano Panazza, *La pittura bresciana del Rinascimento. Catalogo della mostra. Città di Brescia.* Bergamo, 1939.

Lelio Orsi. Exhibition catalogue. Revised by R. Savini and A.M. Chiodi. Reggio Emilia, 1950.

Levey, M., *Painting in XVIII Century Venice.* London, 1959.

Levey M., *Tiepolo and his Age.* Off-print from *Arts and Ideas in Eighteenth-Century Italy.* Rome, 1960.

Lomazzo, G. P., *Trattato dell'arte della pittura.* Milan, 1585.

Arte Lombarda dai Visconti agli Sforza. Palazzo Reale. Milan, 1958. Exhibition catalogue.

Longhi, R., Cose bresciane del Cinquecento. *L'Arte*, XX, 1917, pp. 99—114.

Longhi, R., Il trio dei veronesi. Bassetti, Turchi, Ottini. *Vita Artistica*, 1926.

Longhi, R., Di un libro sul Romanino. *L'Arte*, XXIX, 1926, pp. 144—152.
Longhi, R., *Precisioni nelle Gallerie Italiane. I. Reale Galleria Borghese*. Rome, 1928.
Longhi, R., *Viatico per cinque secoli di pittura veneziana*. Florence, 1946.
Longhi, R., R. Cipriani and G. Testori, *I pittori della realtà in Lombardia*. Milan, 1953.
Longhi, R., Un apice espressionistico di Liberale da Verona. *Paragone*, VI, No. 65, 1955, pp. 3—7.
Lorenzetti, G., *Cà Rezzonico*. Venice, 1936.
Lorenzetti, G., *Feste e maschere veneziani*. Exhibition catalogue. Venice, 1937.
Lorenzetti, G. with the collaboration of G. Mariacher, *Mostra del Tiepolo*. Exhibition catalogue. Venice, 1951.
Lorenzetti, G., *Venezia e il suo estuario*. Venice, 1956.
Lugt, F., *Les Marques de collections*. Amsterdam, 1921.
Lugt, F., *Les Marques de collections*. Supplement. The Hague, 1956.
Lugt, F., J.Q. van Regteren Altena and J.C. Ebbinge Wubben, *Le dessin italien dans les collections hollandaises*. Exhibition catalogue, Vols. I—II. Paris, Rotterdam, Haarlem, 1962.
Magagnato, L., *Disegni del Museo Civico di Bassano. Catalogo della mostra*. Venice, 1956.
Magagnato, L., *Da Altichiero a Pisanello. Museo di Castelvecchio. Verona*. Exhibition catalogue. Venice, 1958.
Mahon, D., *Studies in Seicento Art and Theory*. London, 1947.
Malaguzzi-Valeri, F., *I disegni della R. Pinacoteca di Brera*. Milan, 1906.
Mariacher, G., Gaspare e Antonio Diziani a Cà Rezzonico. *Arte Veneta*, V, 1951, pp. 173—176.
Mariacher, G., *Il Museo Correr di Venezia. I dipinti dal XIV. al XVI. secolo*. Venice, 1957.
Mariette, P.J., *Abecedario de P. J. Mariette et autres notes inédites de cet amateur sur les arts et les artistes*. Paris, 1851—1860, Vols. I—VI.
Marini, R., Non è Giorgionesco il primo Tiziano. *Emporium*, CXXVII, July, 1958, pp. 3—16.
Matteucci, A. M., L'attività veneziana di Bernardo Strozzi. *Arte Veneta*, IX, 1955, pp. 138—154.
Mauroner, F., *Le incisioni di Tiziano*. Venice, 1941.
Meder, J., *Die Handzeichnung, ihre Technik und Entwicklung*. Vienna, 1923.
Meder, J., Tintorettos erster Entwurf zum "Paradies" im Dogenpalaste. *Die Graphischen Künste*, LIV, 1931, pp. 75—80.
Meder, J., Tintorettos erster Entwurf zum "Paradies" und andere Zeichnungen seiner Hand. *Die Graphischen Künste*. Vienna, LVI, 1933, pp. 1—6.
S. Meller, 1911 = Meller, S., *Külföldi mesterek rajzai, XIV—XVIII. sz.* [The Drawings of Old Masters, XIV—XVIII. Centuries]. Exhibition catalogue of the Department of Prints and Drawings, Budapest, 1911.
Meller, S., *Az Esterházy Képtár története* [The History of the Esterházy Collection]. Budapest, 1915.
Michelini, P., Domenico Fetti a Venezia. *Arte Veneta*, IX, 1955, pp. 123—137.
Molmenti, P., *Acque-forti dei Tiepolo*. Venice, 1896.
Molmenti, P., *La storia di Venezia nella vita privata dalle origini alla caduta della Republica*, I—III. Bergamo, 1905.
Molmenti, P., *G.B. Tiepolo*. Milan, 1909.
Mongan, A., Venetian Drawings in America. *Venezia e l'Europa*, 1955, pp. 303—305.
Mongan—Sachs, 1946 = Mongan, A. and P. J. Sachs, Fogg Museum of Art. *Drawings in the Fogg Museum of Art*. Vols. I—II. Cambridge, Mass., 1946.
Morassi, A., Un libro di disegni e due quadri di Sebastiano Ricci. *Cronaca d'Arte*, 1926, p. 256.
Morassi, A., I pittori alla corte di Bernardo Clesio. *Bollettino d'Arte*, IX, 1929—1930, pp. 241—264.
Morassi, A., Francesco Fontebasso a Trento. *Bollettino d'Arte*, XXV, 1931, pp. 119—131.
Morassi, A., The Other Painter of Malpaga. *The Burlington Magazine*, LVIII, 1931, pp. 118—129.
Morassi, A., Opere ignote o inedite di Paolo Veronese. *Bollettino d'Arte*, XXIX, 1935, pp. 249—258.
Morassi, A., *Disegni antichi della Collezione Rasini a Milano*. Milan, 1937.

Morassi, A., *Brescia. Catalogo delle cose d'arte e di antichità d'Italia*, Vol. XI. Rome, 1939.

Morassi, A., Giambattista e Domenico Tiepolo alla Villa Valmarana. *Le Arti*, April-May, 1941.

Morassi, A., *Tiepolo e la Villa Valmarana*. Milan, 1945.

Morassi, A., Esordi di Tiziano. *Arte Veneta*, VIII, 1954, pp. 178—198.

Morassi, A., Un disegno e un dipinto sconosciuti di Giorgione. *Emporium*, LXI, 1955, pp. 146—159.

Morassi, A., *G. B. Tiepolo*. London, 1955.

Morassi, A., *Dessins vênitiens du dix-huitième siècle de la Collection du Duc de Talleyrand*. Milan, 1958.

Morassi, A., Pellegrini e Guardi. *Emporium*, CXXVII, November, 1958, pp. 194—212.

Morassi, A., *Alcuni disegni inediti del Romanino*. Studies in honour of Karl M. Swoboda. Vienna, 1959.

Morassi, A., *Disegni veneti del Settecento nella Collezione Paul Wallraf*. Catalogo della mostra. Venice, 1959.

Morassi, A., Documenti, pitture e disegni inediti dello Zuccarelli. *Emporium*, 1960.

Morassi, A., *A Complete Catalogue of the Paintings of G.B. Tiepolo*. London, 1963.

Mortari, L., Su Bernardo Strozzi. *Bollettino d'Arte*, XL, 1955, pp. 311—333.

Moschini, G. A., *Della letteratura veneziana del secolo XVIII etc.* Venice, 1806.

Moschini, G. A., *Nuova guida di Venezia*. Venice, 1847.

Moschini, V., I disegni del '700 alla mostra di Venezia. *Dedalo*, X, Fasc. V, 1929, V, pp. 301—330.

Moschini, V., Disegni del tardo '500 e del '600 all'Accademia di Venezia. *Bollettino d'Arte*, XXV, 1931, pp. 70—83.

Moschini, V., *La pittura italiana del Settecento*. Florence, 1931.

Moschini, V., *Francesco Guardi*. Milan, 1952.

Moschini, V., *Canaletto*. Milan, 1954.

Moschini, V., Inediti di Palma il Giovane e compagni. *Arte Veneta*, XII, 1958, p. 97.

M. Mrozinska, 1958 = Mrozinska, M. *Disegni veneti in Polonia*. Exhibition catalogue. Venice, 1958.

Mrozinska, M., *I disegni del Codice Bonola del Museo di Varsavia*. Exhibition catalogue. Venice, 1959.

Mucchi, A. M., e C. Della Croce, *Il pittore Andrea Celesti*. Milan, 1954.

M. Muraro, 1953 = Muraro, M., *Mostra di disegni veneziani del Sei- e Settecento*. Exhibition catalogue. *Gabinetto Disegni e Stampe degli Uffizi*. Florence, 1953.

M. Muraro, 1957 = Muraro, M., *Catalogo della Mostra di Disegni veneti della collezione János Scholz*. Exhibition catalogue. Venice, 1957.

Muraro, M., Un'Adorazione dei Pastori affrescata da Domenico Campagnola a Vicenza. *Emporium*, CXXX, July, 1959, pp. 3—8.

Muraro, M., Giuseppe Zais e un "Giovin Signore" nelle pitture murali di Strà. *Emporium*, LXVI, November, 1960, pp. 195—218.

Muraro, M., Notes on Old and Modern Drawings. The Drawings of Giovanni Antonio Pellegrini. *The Art Quarterly*, Winter, 1960, pp. 359—370.

Muraro, M., Giulio Carpioni. *Acropoli*, 1960—1961, pp. 67—78.

Murr, Ch. Th., *Description du Cabinet de Monsieur Paul de Praun à Nuremberg*. Nuremberg, 1797.

Neumeyer, A., *Drawings from Lombardy and Adjacent Areas 1480—1620*. Mills College Art Gallery, Oakland, 1956. (Exhibition catalogue of the drawings from the János Scholz Collection, New York.)

Neumeyer, A., *Venetian Drawings 1400—1630*. Mills College Art Gallery, Oakland, 1959. (Exhibition catalogue of the drawings from the János Scholz Collection, New York.)

Neumeyer, A., *Venetian Drawings 1600—1800.* Mills College Art Gallery, Oakland, 1960. (Exhibition Catalogue of the drawings from the János Scholz Collection, New York.)

Nicodemi, G., *Pittori Lombardi.* Rome, 1922.

Nicodemi, G., *Gerolamo Romanino.* Brescia, 1925.

Nicolson, B., Di alcuni dipinti veneziani nelle collezioni reali d'Inghilterra. *Arte Veneta,* I, 1947, pp. 222—226.

Oberhuber, K., *Parmigianino und sein Kreis. Ausstellung der Graphischen Sammlung Albertina.* Vienna, 1963.

Oldenburg, R., *Domenico Fetti.* Rome, 1921.

Orlandi, P. A. Ab., *Abecedario pittorico.* Venice, 1753.

Pallucchini, R., *Mostra di Paolo Veronese.* Exhibition catalogue. Venice, 1939.

Pallucchini, R., *Gli incisori veneti del Settecento.* Venice, 1941.

Pallucchini, R., *I disegni de Giambattista Pittoni.* Padua, 1945.

Pallucchini, R., *Gli affreschi di Giambattista e Giandomenico Tiepolo alla Villa Valmarana di Vicenza.* Bergamo, 1945.

Pallucchini, R., *I capolavori dei musei veneti.* Exhibition catalogue. Venice, 1946.

Pallucchini, R., Postilla per Gaspare Diziani. *Arte Veneta,* II, 1948, pp. 135—138.

Pallucchini, R., *Mostra di Giovanni Bellini.* Exhibition catalogue. Venice, 1949.

Pallucchini, R., *La Giovinezza del Tintoretto.* Milan, 1950.

Pallucchini, R., *Lezioni di storia dell'arte... La pittura veneziana del Settecento,* I. Bologna, 1951.

Pallucchini, R., Studi Ricceschi (I). Contributo a Sebastiano. *Arte Veneta,* VI, 1952, pp. 63—84.

Pallucchini, R., Modelli di G.A. Pellegrini. *Arte Veneta,* VII, 1953, pp. 107—110.

Pallucchini, R., Studi Ricceschi (II). Contributo a Marco. *Arte Veneta,* IX, 1955, pp. 171—198.

Pallucchini, R., Un soffitto ritrovato di Francesco Fontebasso. *Arte Veneta,* XI, 1957, pp. 162—167.

Pallucchini, R., I disegni veneti della Collezione Scholz esposti all'Istituto di Storia dell'Arte della Fondazione Cini. *Arte Veneta,* XI, 1957, pp. 255—256.

Pallucchini, R., Disegni oxfordiani e polacchi a San Giorgio. *Arte Veneta,* XII, 1958, pp. 258—259.

Pallucchini, R., *Giovanni Bellini.* Milan, 1959.

Pallucchini, R., Una mostra di disegni del Pellegrini. *Arte Veneta,* XIII—XIV, 1959—1960, pp. 297—298.

Pallucchini, R., *La pittura veneziana del Settecento.* Venice, Rome, 1960.

Pallucchini, R., Novità ed appunti per Giovanni Antonio Pellegrini. *Pantheon,* XVIII, 1960, I, pp. 182—191, II, 245—253.

Pallucchini, R., Altri soffitti del Fontebasso. *Arte Veneta,* XV, 1961, pp. 182—191.

Pallucchini, R., Studi Tizianeschi. *Arte Veneta,* XV, 1961, pp. 286—295.

Panofsky, E., *Hercules am Scheidewege.* Leipzig, 1930.

Panofsky, E., Das erste Blatt aus dem "Libro" Giorgio Vasaris. *Städel-Jahrbuch,* VI, 1930, pp. 25—72.

Panofsky, E., *The Iconography of Correggio's Camera di San Paolo.* London, 1961.

Parker, K. T., *North Italian Drawings of the Quattrocento.* London, 1927.

Parker, K. T., Nuovi disegni veneti al Museo Ashmolean di Oxford. *Arte Veneta,* I, 1947, pp. 47—48.

K.T. Parker, 1956 = K.T. Parker, *Catalogue of the Collection of Drawings in the Ashmolean Museum,* Vol. II: *Italian Schools.* Oxford, 1956.

K. T. Parker, 1958 = K.T. Parker, *Disegni veneti di Oxford. Catalogo della mostra.* Venice, 1958.

Parker, K. T. e J. Byam Shaw, *Canaletto e Guardi.* Exhibition catalogue. Venice, 1962.

Pevsner, N., Giulio Cesare Procaccini. *Rivista d'Arte,* XI, 1929, pp. 322—354.

Pigler, A., *Országos Szépművészeti Múzeum. A Régi Képtár katalógusa* [Museum of Fine Arts in Budapest. Catalogue of the Old Picture Gallery]. Budapest, 1954.

Pigler, A., *Barockthemen,* I—II. Budapest, 1956.

Pigler, A., Un gruppo i dipinti di Francesco Fontebasso a Budapest. *Arte Veneta*, XIII—XIV, 1959—1960, pp. 155—161.
Pignatti, T., Venetian Seicento and Settecento Drawings. An Uffizi Exhibition. *The Burlington Magazine*, XCVI, 1954, pp. 309—314.
Pignatti, T., Drawings from the Museo Civico Bassano. *The Burlington Magazine*, XCVIII, 1956, pp. 373—374.
Pignatti, T., Disegni inediti di Zuccarelli e Zais al Museo Correr. *Arte Veneta*, X, 1956, pp. 177—182.
Pignatti, T., Venetian Drawings of the Scholz Collection. *The Burlington Magazine*, XCIX, 1957, pp. 385—386.
Pignatti, T., *Il quaderno di disegni del Canaletto alle Gallerie di Venezia.* Milan, 1958.
Pignatti, T., Pellegrini Drawings in Venice. *The Burlington Magazine*, CI, 1959, pp. 451—452.
Pignatti, T., *La mostra della pittura del Seicento a Venezia.* Catalogo dei disegni. Venice, 1959.
Pignatti, T., *Il Museo Correr di Venezia. Dipinti del XVII. e XVIII. secolo.* Catalogue. Venice, 1960.
Pignatti, T., *Eighteenth-Century Venetian Drawings from the Correr Museum.* Circulated by the Shmithsonian Institution 1963—1964.
Pilo, G. M., Le prime opere datate di F. Zugno. *Arte Veneta*, X, 1956, pp. 201—203.
Pilo, G. M., Ritrovamenti per Francesco Zugno. *Paragone*, 1959, III, p. 33.
Pilo, G. M., Francesco Zugno. *Saggi e Memorie di Storia dell'Arte*, II. Venice, 1959, pp. 325—378.
Pilo, G. M., Ricci, Pellegrini, Amigoni: Nuovi appunti su un rapporto vicendevole. *Arte Antica e Moderna.* 1960. No. 10, pp. 174—189.
Pilo, G.M., Otto nuove acquaforti ed altre aggiunte grafiche a Marco Ricci. *Arte Veneta*, XV, 1961, pp. 165—174.
Pilo, G. M., *Carpioni.* Venice, 1961.
Pilo, G. M., *Marco Ricci.* Exhibition Catalogue in Bassano del Grappa. Venice, 1963.
Pinetti, A., *Inventario degli oggetti d'arte d'Italia. I. Provincia dei Bergamo.* Rome, 1931.
Pittaluga, M., Le acqueforti di Marco Ricci. *Emporium*, 1946, No. 3.
Pittaluga, M., *Acquafortisti veneziani del Settecento.* Florence, 1952.
Popham, A.E., *Italian Drawings Exhibited at the Royal Academy.* Burlington House. London, 1930.
Popham, A.E., and Ph. Pouncey, *Italian Drawings in the Department of Prints and Drawings in the British Museum. The Fourteenth and Fifteenth Centuries.* Catalogue, Vols. I—II. London, 1950.
Popham, A.E., Disegni veneziani acquistati recentemente dal British Museum. *Arte Veneta*, I, 1947, pp. 226—230.
Popham—Wilde, 1949 = Popham, A. E., and J. Wilde, *The Italian Drawings... at Windsor Castle.* London, 1949.
Popham, A. E., *The Drawings of Parmigianino.* London, 1953.
Popham, A. E., *Correggio's Drawings.* London, 1957.
Popham, A. E., Dessins du Parmesan au Musée des Beaux-Arts. *Bulletin du Musée National Hongrois des Beaux-Arts.* Budapest, 1961, No. 19, pp. 43—58.
Popham, A. E., *Old Master Drawings from Chatsworth. USA.* Exhibition catalogue, 1962—1963.
Prijatelj, K., Le opere del Palma il Giovine e dei manieristi veneziani in Dalmazia. Venezia e l'Europa. *Atti del XVIII. Congresso Internazionale di Storia dell'Arte.* Venice, 1956, p. 294.
Puerari, A., *Mostra di antiche pitture dal XIV. al XIX. sec.* Exhibition catalogue. Cremona, 1948.
Puppi, L., La formazione vicentina di Francesco Bonsignori. *Vita Veronese*, IX, 1958, pp. 170—172.
L. Puppi, Arte Veneta, 1959—1960 = L. Puppi, Disegni veneti al Museo di Belle Arti di Budapest. *Arte Veneta*, XIII—XIV, 1959—1960, pp. 288—291.

Puppi, L., Nota sui disegni del Fogolino. *Arte Veneta*, XV, 1961, pp. 223—227.

Puppi, L., *Bartolomeo Montagna*. Venice, 1962.

Puppi, L., Angelo Zotto et quelques fresques padouanes du XVe siècle. *Bulletin du Musée National Hongrois des Beaux-Arts*, No. 21. Budapest, 1962, pp. 31—43, Plates 20—21.

A. O. Quintavalle, 1948 = Quintavalle, A.O., *Il Parmigianino*. Milan, 1948.

Ragghianti, C. L., *Antichi disegni e stampe dell'Accademia Carrara di Bergamo*. Bergamo, 1963.

Ragghianti, C. L., Sul metodo nello studio dei disegni. *Le Arti*, 1940.

Rearick, W.R., Battista Franco and the Grimani Chapel. *Saggi e Memorie di Storia dell'Arte*, II. Venice, 1959. pp. 105—139.

Ricci, C., *La scenografia italiana*. Milan, 1930.

Riccoboni, A., Antonio Zanchi pittore veneto. *Rassegna d'Arte*, 1922, p. 109.

Riccoboni, A., *Pittura veneta. Prima mostra d'arte antica delle raccolte private veneziane*. Exhibition catalogue. Venice, 1947.

Ridolfi, C., *Le maraviglie dell'arte*, Venice, 1648. Edited by Detlev Freiherr von Hadeln. Parte prima: Berlin, 1914. Parte seconda: Berlin, 1924.

Rizzi, A., Opere inedite di Gaspare Diziani nel Friuli. *Acropoli*, Annual Set No. II, 1961, p. 111.

Sack, E., *Giambattista und Domenico Tiepolo*. Hamburg, 1910.

Salmina, L., Disegni di G. B. Tiepolo all' Ermitage. *Arte Veneta*, XI, 1957, pp. 143—151.

Salmina, L., Neue Zuschreibungen an Marco Marcola. Сообщения Государственного Эрмитажа. Leningrad, 1960, XVIII, pp. 33—35.

Salmina, L., Studien über venezianische Zeichnungen des XVII. bis XIX. Jahrhunderts. Die Zeichnungen des P.A. Novelli in der Ermitage. Труды Государственного Эрмитажа. Leningrad, 1961, VI, pp. 153—174.

Salmina, L., Alcuni disegni veneziani del sec. XVIII. nella collezione dell'Ermitage. *Acta Historiae Artium Academiae Scientiarum Hungaricae*, Vol. IX, Fasc. 1—2, 1963, pp. 171—189.

Salmina, L., *Disegni veneti del Museo di Leningrado*. Exhibition Catalogue. Venice, 1964.

Schendel, A. van, *Le dessin en Lombardie*. Brussels, 1938.

Scheyer, E., A Drawing Attributed to Giovanni Antonio Pellegrini in Detroit. *Pantheon*, VIII, 1960, pp. 153—156.

Schilling, E., Eine Zeichnung Giorgiones. *Festschrift für M.L. Friedländer*, 1927.

Schlosser, J. V., Zwei Kapitel aus der Biographie einer Stadt. 1. Die Entstehung Venedigs. 2. Venedig im 18. Jahrhundert. Written 1897, Published in *Präludien*. Berlin, 1927, pp. 82—159.

Schlosser, J. v., *La letteratura artistica*. Edited by Otto Kurz. Florence, Vienna, 1956.

Schmitt, U.B., Francesco Bonsignori. *Münchner Jahrbuch der Bildenden Kunst*. Dritte Folge, Vol. XII, 1961. Off-print, pp. 73—152.

Scholz, J., Notes on Drawings by Francesco Fontebasso. *L'Arte*, July, 1948—July, 1951, p. 40.

Scholz, J., Notes on Drawings on Brescian Renaissance Drawings. *Essays in Honor of Hans Tietze*. Extrait de la *Gazette des Beaux-Arts*. New York, 1958.

Scholz, J., *Baroque and Romantic Stage Design*. New York, 1962.

Scholz, J., Notes on Old and Modern Drawings. *The Art Quarterly*. XXIII, 1960, pp. 52—68.

Schönbrunner—Meder, Albertina Publication = Schönbrunner, J. and J. Meder, *Handzeichnungen alter Meister aus der Albertina und anderen Sammlungen*. Vienna, 1896—1908.

Seicento a Venezia. La pittura del Seicento a Venezia. Exhibition catalogue. Revised by P. Zampetti, G. Mariacher, G. M. Pilo. Catalogue of the Drawings by T. Pignatti. Venice, 1959.

Seilern, A., *Italian Paintings and Drawings at 56, Princes Gate, London, SW7*. London, 1959.

Selvatico, P., *Storia... delle arti del disegno*. Venice, 1852.

Semenzato, C., Giuseppe Bernardi detto il Torretto. *Arte Veneta*, XII, 1958, pp. 169—178.

Serra, L. (Laudedeo Testi, Giovanni Copertini), *Inventario degli oggetti d'arte d'Italia*, III: *Provincia di Parma*. Rome, 1934.

Serra, L. (Guglielmo Matthiae), *Inventario degli ogetti d'arte d'Italia*, VI: *Provincia di Mantova.* Rome, 1935.

Suida, W., Studien zur lombardischen Malerei. *Monatshefte für Kunstwissenschaft*, 1909, p. 472.

Temanza, T., *Vita dei più celebri architetti e scultori veneziani che fiorirono nel secolo Decimosesto.* Venice, 1778.

Temanza, T., *Zibaldon di memorie storiche appartenenti a Professori delle Belle Arti del Disegno*, Manoscritto n. 796 della Biblioteca de Seminario Patriarcale di Venezia, Cod. No. CCLXI. M.U.3.

Tietze, H., *Tizian*, Vols. I—II. Vienna, 1936.

Tietze-Conrat, E., Echte und unechte Tintoretto-Zeichnungen. *Die Graphischen Künste.* Neue Folge, I, 1936, pp. 88—100 and 140.

Tietze, H., Tizian-Studien. *Jahrbuch der Kunsthistorischen Sammlungen in Wien.* Vienna, neue Folge, Vol. X, 1936, pp. 137—192.

Tietze, H. and E. Tietze-Conrat, Contributi critici allo studio organico dei disegni veneziani del Cinquecento. *La Critica d'Arte*, VII, 1937, pp. 77—88.

Tietze, H. und E. Tietze-Conrat, Tizian-Graphik. *Die Graphischen Künste*, Vol. III, 1938, pp. 52—71.

Tietze, H., Master and Workshop in the Venetian Renaissance. *Parnassus*, 1940.

Tietze, H. and E. Tietze-Conrat, On Several Drawings Erroneously Attributed to Tizian. *Gazette des Beaux-Arts*, XXII, 1942, pp. 115—121.

Tietzes, 1944 = Tietze, H. and E. Tietze-Conrat, *The Drawings of the Venetian Painters in the 15th and 16th Centuries.* New York, 1944.

Tietze, H. and E. Tietze-Conrat, Venetian Drawings in the Hermitage. *The Art Bulletin*, 1945, XXVII, pp. 149—151.

Tietze, H., *European Master Drawings in the United States.* New York, 1947.

Tietze, H., *Tintoretto.* London, 1948.

Tietze, H., Nuovi disegni veneti del Cinquecento in collezioni americane. *Arte Veneta*, II, 1948, pp. 56—66.

Tintelnot, H., *Barocktheater und barocke Kunst.* Berlin, 1939.

Tintoretto. Exhibition catalogue. Venice, 1937.

Tiziano. Exhibition catalogue. Venice, 1935.

Toesca, O., *La pittura e la miniatura nella Lombardia.* Milan, 1912, p. 452.

Tolnay, Ch. de, *History and Technique of Old Master Drawings.* New York, 1943.

Tolnay, Ch. de, L'interpretazione dei cicli pittorici del Tintoretto nella Scuola di San Rocco. *Critica d'Arte*, 41, September-October, 1960, pp. 341—376.

Trecca, G., *Catalogo della Pinacoteca Communale.* Bergamo, 1912, No. 217.

Valcanover, F., *Mostra di pitture del Settecento nel Bellunese.* (Prefazione di G. Fiocco.) Exhibition catalogue. Venice, 1954.

Vayer, L., *Master Drawings.* Budapest, 1957.

Velencei... rajzok, 1960 = Fenyő, I., *Velencei és egyéb északitáliai rajzok* [Venetian and other North Italian Drawings]. Exhibition catalogue of the Department of Prints and Drawings, 1960.

Venturi, A., *Storia dell'Arte italiana. La pittura del Quattrocento*, Vol. VII, Parte I, 1911. Parte III, 1914. Parte IV, 1915. *La pittura del Cinquecento*, Vol. IX, Parte II, 1926. Parte III, 1928. Parte IV, 1929. Parte VI, 1933.

Venturi, L., *Giorgione e il Giorgionismo.* Milan, 1913.

Viale, M., Disegni dei Galliari per "La vittoria d'Imeneo". *Bollettino della Società Piemontese di Archeologia e Belle Arti*, 1950—1951.

Viale, M., Pensieri e disegni di Fabrizio Galliari in relazione a gusto neoclassico. *Palladio*, 1952.

Viale, M., *Disegni scenografici dei Galliari. Museo Civico di Torino.* Turin, 1956.

Viale, M., I disegni scenografici della raccolta Fatio. *Critica d'Arte*, IV, Fasc. 19—24, 1957. pp. 370—395.
Viale, M., *La scenografia del Settecento e i fratelli Galliari.* Turin, 1963.
Vigni, G., *Disegni del Tiepolo.* Padova, 1942.
Vigni, G., Note sull'attività del Tiepolo a Madrid e a Würzburg e sul Quaderno Correr. Venezia e l'Europa. *Atti del XVIII. Congresso Internazionale di Storia dell'Arte.* Venice, 1956, p. 362.
Voss, H., Studien zur venezianischen Vedutenmalerei des 18. Jahrhunderts. *Repertorium für Kunstwissenschaft*, Vol. XLVII, 1926, pp. 1—45.
Voss, H., *Zeichnungen der italienischen Spätrenaissance.* Munich, 1928.
Voss, H., Die Flucht nach Ägypten. *Saggi e Memorie di Storia dell'Arte*, I, 1957, pp. 27—61.
Watson, F. J. B., *Eighteenth Century Venice. An Exhibition of Paintings and Drawings held at the Whitechapel Art Gallery.* (Catalogue.) London, 1951.
Watson, F. J. B., A Venetian Settecento Chapel in the English Countryside. *Arte Veneta*, VIII, 1954, pp. 295—302.
Watson, F. J. B., English Villas and Venetian Decorators. *The Journal of the Royal Institute of the British Architects*, 1954.
Watson, F. J. B., La mostra di pitture settecentesca di Belluno. *Arte Veneta*, IX, 1955, pp. 248—264.
Watson, F. J. B., English Taste in the Eighteenth Century. *The Connoisseur*, 1956, pp. 102—105 and 124.
Weigel, R., *Die Werke der Maler in ihren Handzeichnungen.* Leipzig, 1865.
Wickhoff, F., *Die italienischen Handzeichnungen der Albertina*, Vol. I: *Die Venezianischen, die Lombardischen und die Bolognesischen Schulen.* Beiheft zum Jahrbuch der Sammlungen des Allerhöchsten Kaiserhauses, XII, 1891. Vol. II: *Die Römische Schule.* Beiheft zum Jahrbuch der Sammlungen des Allerhöchsten Kaiserhauses, XIII, 1892.
Wilde, J., Die Probleme um Domenico Mancini. *Jahrbuch der Kunsthist. Sammlungen in Wien.* Vienna, 1933.
Wilde, J., Über einige venezianische Frauenbildnisse der Renaissance. *Festschrift für Alexis Petrovics.* Budapest, 1934.
Zampetti, P., Affreschi inediti di Marcello Fogolino. *Arte Veneta*, I, 1947, pp. 217—222.
Zampetti, P., Inediti di Bernardo Strozzi. *Emporium*, 1949, p. 17.
Zampetti, P., *Catalogo della Mostra della Pittura Veneta nella Marche.* Bergamo, 1950.
Zampetti, P., *Lorenzo Lotto.* Exhibition Catalogue. Venice, 1953.
Zampetti, P., *Giorgione e i Giorgioneschi.* Exhibition catalogue. Venice, 1955.
Zampetti, P., Postille alla mostra di Giorgione. *Arte Veneta*, IX, 1955, pp. 54—70.
Zanetti, A. M., *Descrizione di tutte le pubbliche pitture della città di Venezia ecc. ossia rinnovazione delle Ricche Minere di Marco Boschini.* Venice, 1733.
Zanetti, A. M., *Della pittura veneziana e delle opere pubbliche dei veneziani maestri.* Venice, 1771.
Zani, P., *Enciclopedia delle Belle Arti.* Parma, 1819.
Zannandreis-Biadego, *Le vite dei pittori, scultori e architetti veronesi.* Verona—Padua, 1891.
Zanotto, F., *Venezia e le sue lagune.* Venice, 1847.
Zanotto, F., *Storia della pittura veneziana.* Venice, 1837.

LIST OF FIGURES

1 Francesco Bonsignori (?): The Madonna and Child with Angels Playing Music. Verso of Plate 4

2 Francesco Bonsignori (?): St. Christopher. Verso of Plate 5

3 Francesco Bonsignori: Madonna with Saints. Altarpiece from S. Fermo Maggiore. Verona, Museo di Castelvecchio

4 Liberale da Verona: Madonna and Child. London, National Gallery

5 Anonymous, Venice, end of the fifteenth century: Sheet with astrological (?) symbols. Verso of Plate 6

6 Anonymous, Venice, end of the fifteenth century: A sheet of sketches. Rotterdam, Museum Boymans-van Beuningen

7 Verso of Fig. 6

8 Anonymous, Venice, about 1500: Study of garment. Verso of Plate 8

9 Marco Basaiti: Detail from "Christ on the Mount of Olives." Venice, Accademia

10 Bernardino Luini: Study of drapery. Verso of Plate 9

11 Romanino: The Nativity. Brescia, Pinacoteca Tosio e Martinengo

12 Correggio: Christ Enthroned in Clouds. Verso of Plate 17

13 Camillo Boccaccino: Madonna and Saints. Prague, Narodní Galerie

14 Parmigianino: St. Cecilia and David. Organ wing of the Church of Steccata at Parma

15 Enea Vico: Proserpina. After Parmigianino. Engraving

16 Malosso: Madonna and Saints. Cremona, Museo Civico

17 Moncalvo: The Birth of the Virgin. Pavia, Museo Civico

18 Morazzone: An Angel Playing Music. Verso of Plate 76

19 G. Ferroni's engraving after Morazzone. Cf. Plate 77

20 J.C. Loth: Philemon and Baucis. Vienna, Kunsthistorisches Museum

21 Pietro Liberi: The Death of Adonis. Padua, Palazzo Conti

22 Anonymous, Northern Italy, beginning of the seventeenth century: Study of a head. Budapest, Museum of Fine Arts

23 Anonymous, Northern Italy, beginning of the seventeenth century: Study of a head. Budapest, Museum of Fine Arts

24 G.B. Castiglione: Figure of a Frightened Man in two variants. Verso of Plate 94

25 G.B. Pittoni: Sketches of heads and figures in indian ink. Verso of Plate 104

26 G.B. Pittoni: Sketches of figures in pencil and indian ink. Verso of Plate 102

27 Anton Kern: A copy after Pittoni. Budapest, Museum of Fine Arts

28 Gaspare Diziani: The Massacre of the Innocents. Venice, S. Stefano

29 Gaspare Diziani: A Man with a Dagger. Verso of Plate 110

30 Gaspare Diziani: Aeneas and Anchises. Venice, Museo Correr

31 Gaspare Diziani: The Assumption of the Virgin. Budapest, Museum of Fine Arts

32 Gaspare Diziani (?): Minerva. Venice, Museo Correr

33 Giuseppe Bazzani: The Raising of Lazarus. Whereabouts unknown

34 Giuseppe Zais: Cavalry Battle. Budapest, Museum of Fine Arts

LIST OF PLATES

1 Anonymous, Lombardy or Bologna, beginning of the fifteenth century: Hunting Adventure
2—3 Anonymous, Lombardy, about 1440: The pages of a sketch-book with animal figures
4 Francesco Bonsignori (?): The Madonna and Child with Angels Playing Music. Beneath two saints
5 Francesco Bonsignori (?): The Madonna and Child, with a five-headed dragon beneath the group
6 Anonymous, Venice, end of the fifteenth century: Sheet with astrological (?) symbols
7 Follower of Mantegna, about 1500: The Construction of the Argo
8 Anonymous, Venice, about 1500: Recumbent Woman, Mary (?)
9 Bernardino Luini: Seated Woman
10 Bartolomeo Montagna: The Madonna and Child
11 Gaudenzio Ferrari: The Four Evangelists
12 Giorgione: St. Elizabeth with the Infant St. John
13 Girolamo Romanino: The Nativity
14 Girolamo Romanino: Group of Armed Riders
15 Anonymous, Padua or Ferrara, about 1520: A Group with the Virgin from a Crucifixion
16 Correggio: Madonna Enthroned in Clouds
17 Correggio: Christ Enthroned in Clouds
18 Correggio: Composition with Two Female Figures
19 Bernardino Gatti: Study of the Virgin
20 Giovanni Battista Franco: Design to a historical (?) scene
21 Anonymous, Venice, end of the sixteenth century: The Bearing of the Cross
22 Domenico Campagnola: David and Goliath
23 Follower of Domenico Campagnola: Mountainous Landscape with Antique Ruins
24 After Titian (Domenico Campagnola?): Landscape with Woods and Town
25 Anonymous, Venice, sixteenth century (Domenico Campagnola?), with corrections by Rembrandt: Hilly Landscape with Houses and a Water-Mill
26 Camillo Boccaccino: A Holy Bishop
27 Unknown follower of Giorgione, about 1530: Dancing Figures in Landscape
28 Parmigianino: Two studies of a David figure. Verso of the following drawing
29 Parmigianino: St. Cecilia
30 Parmigianino: A Woman Seated at a Table
31 Verso of Plate 30: Two Female Nudes
32 Parmigianino: Proserpina Changing Ascalaphus into an Owl
33 Parmigianino: Two Models
34 Parmigianino: Venus with Cupid and Female Nudes
35 Schiavone: Study of a draped female figure
36 Schiavone: The Martyrdom of St. Catherine

37 Lelio Orsi: The Creation of the World
38—39 Lelio Orsi: Joseph Cast into the Well by His Brothers
40 Luca Cambiaso: The Holy Family in Front of a House
41 Luca Cambiaso: Madonna and Child with the Infant St. John and St. Catherine
42 Luca Cambiaso: The Three Theological Virtues
43 Luca Cambiaso: The Last Judgement
44 Bernardo Castello: Battle Scene
45 Bernardo Castello: Scene in a Camp
46 Jacopo Tintoretto: Study after the so-called 'Atlas'
47 Verso of Plate 46: A variant of the same subject
48 Jacopo Tintoretto: Two studies after the so-called 'Atlas'
49 Verso of Plate 48: Study after the same figure
50 Jacopo Tintoretto or his workshop: Man Bending, Seen from the Back
51 Jacopo Tintoretto, workshop: The Emperor Vitellius
52 Antonio Badile: Madonna Enthroned with SS. Peter and Paul
53 Andrea Palladio and Paolo Veronese: Design for a tomb
54 Paolo Veronese: Peter of Amiens before the Doge Vitale Michiel
55 Verso of Plate 54: A traced variant of the same scene
56 Paolo Veronese: The Execution of a Martyr (?) and other sketches
57 Paolo Veronese: Christ in the House of Simon
58 Follower of Veronese (Antonio Vassilacchi, called 'aliense' [?]): The Queen of Sheba before King Solomon
59 Palma il Giovane (?): A sheet of studies
60 Palma il Giovane: The Brazen Serpent
61 Palma il Giovane: A Naval Battle between Turks and Venetians
62a Verso of Plate 60: The Gathering of Manna
62b Verso of Plate 61: The Gathering of Manna
63 Palma il Giovane: St. Jerome
64 Palma il Giovane: Pietà and Head of a Bearded Man. Verso of the following plate
65a Palma il Giovane: The Miracle of the Loaves and Fishes. Recto of the preceding plate
65b Palma il Giovane: The Miracle of the Loaves and Fishes. Painting in the Church of the Carmini in Venice
66 Palma il Giovane: Adoration of the Magi
67 Anonymous, Venice, end of the sixteenth century (Andrea Vicentino?): The Judgement of Paris
68 Anonymous, Venice, about 1600: The Funeral of a Saint
69 Giovanni Battista Trotti (Malosso): St. Homobonus and St. Himerius Commend the Town of Cremona to the Patronage of the Madonna
70 Guglielmo Caccia (Moncalvo): Virgin and Child with St. Anne and the Infant St. John
71 Guglielmo Caccia (Moncalvo): The Birth of the Virgin
72 Giulio Cesare Procaccini: Susannah and the Elders
73 Verso of Plate 72: An Apostle
74 Giulio Cesare Procaccini: Sketches to a "St. Andrew"
75 Verso of Plate 74: Sketches to a composition of "The Last Supper"
76 Pier Francesco Morazzone (P. F. Mazuchelli): St. Francis before the Sultan
77 Pier Francesco Morazzone (P. F. Mazuchelli): The Fire-Ordeal of St. Francis before the Sultan
78 Giovanni Battista Mauro della Rovere (il Fiammenghino): Moses; above him a Putto with a Book and a Serpent
79 Giovanni Battista Mauro della Rovere: Christ Appearing before his Disciples

80 Marcantonio Bassetti: Moses Striking Water from the Rock
81 Domenico Fetti (?): Woman Reading
82 Sebastiano Mazzoni (?): Young Amor Chastised by Nymphs
83 Bernardo Strozzi: Christ and the Woman of Samaria
84 Bernardo Strozzi: Christ in the House of Simon
85 Johann Carl Loth (Carlotto): Jupiter and Mercury with Philemon and Baucis
86 Giulio Carpioni: Clearing in a Forest with a Sleeping Man
87 Giulio Carpioni: A sheet of sketches with bacchantes, a river-god, the Magdalene (?) and other figures
88 Antonio Zanchi (?): Alexander the Great before the Body of Darius
89 Pietro Liberi: The Death of Adonis
90 Anonymous, Northern Italy (Milan?), beginning of the seventeenth century: Head of a Monk
91 Anonymous, Northern Italy (Milan?), beginning of the seventeenth century: Head of a Bishop
92 Giovanni Benedetto Castiglione: Allegory in Honour of the Duchess of Mantua
93 Giovanni Benedetto Castiglione: The Assumption of the Virgin
94 Giovanni Benedetto Castiglione: A sheet of sketches
95 Giovanni Benedetto Castiglione: Fauns Fighting
96 Giovanni Andrea Ansaldo: Allegory of Ferdinand Medici II
97 Bartolomeo Biscaino: The Madonna and Child
98 Anonymous, Venice, beginning of the eighteenth century (Andrea Celesti?): Esther before Ahasuerus
99 Sebastiano Ricci: Hercules at the Cross-Roads
100 Giovanni Battista Marcola: St. Francis before the Sultan
101 Girolamo Brusaferro: The Holy Family Appearing to St. Stephen
102 Giovanni Battista Pittoni: A detail of the composition "The Glorification of Newton"
103 Giovanni Battista Pittoni: The Nativity
104 Giovanni Battista Pittoni: The Adoration of the Magi
105 Gaspare Diziani: The Madonna with St. Nicholas, St. Sebastian and a Third Saint in a Rococo Frame
106 Gaspare Diziani: St. Anthony Kneeling before the Madonna
107 Gaspare Diziani: The Nativity
108 Gaspare Diziani: The Magdalene
109 Gaspare Diziani: Fighting Knights
110 Gaspare Diziani: Aeneas and Anchises
111 Gaspare Diziani: The Raising of the Youth of Nain
112 Gaspare Diziani: Boreas, the God of Winds Abducting Oreithyia
113 Gaspare Diziani: The Rape of Helen
114 Gaspare Diziani (?): Minerva Enthroned on Clouds
115 Verso of Plate 114: A similar representation
116a Gaspare Diziani (?): The Madonna Appearing to St. Francis
116b Gaspare Diziani (?): Design for a monument with the figure of Fame
117 Gaspare Diziani (?): Merchants before the Doge (Sketch to a ceiling)
118 Giovanni Battista Tiepolo: Study of a figure for the fresco on the ceiling of the staircase in the Archbishop's residence at Würzburg
119 Verso of Plate 118: A Study of the Madonna
120 Giovanni Battista Tiepolo: Study
121 Giovanni Battista Tiepolo: A study for the figure of Thetis

122 Giovanni Domenico Tiepolo: Study of a head after Giovanni Battista Tiepolo's painting in the Museum of Fine Arts in Budapest: "St. James of Compostella on Horseback"
123 Giovanni Domenico Tiepolo: The Assumption of the Virgin
124a Francesco Fontebasso: A sheet of studies with the head of a woman and two putti
124b Francesco Fontebasso: A sheet of studies with the head of a bearded man and two hands
125 Giuseppe Bernardi (Torretti): The Second Gondola
126 Giuseppe Bazzani: The Presentation at the Temple
127 Verso of Plate 126: Four studies of heads
128 Marco Ricci: Landscape
129 Bernardo Bellotto (Canaletto): The Porta Pontecorvo and the Church of Sta Giustina at Padua as Seen from the Bastioni
130 Giuseppe Zais: Landscape with a River and a Stone Bridge
131 Francesco Guardi: The Campo SS. Giovanni e Paolo in Venice. Study for the painting of the same subject in the Louvre
132 Giovanni Battista Casanova: Design for a group
133 Francesco Casanova: Study of a Rider
134a,b Antonio Maria di Girolamo Zanetti: The Madonna and Child
135 Giovanni Battista Piranesi: Man Reclining on a Sofa
136 Pietro Antonio Novelli: Portrait of an Artist
137 Pietro Antonio Novelli: The Card-Player
138 Pietro Antonio Novelli: St. Lawrence and an Angel Commend a Venetian Patrician to the Madonna's Protection. Design for an altarpiece
139 Francesco Zugno: Minerva in the Library
140 Fabrizio Galliari: Large Hall, Façade of a Building and Section of a Park. Design for a stage set
141 Fabrizio Galliari: Section of a Park with Arcades. Design for a stage set
142 Lorenzo Sacchetti: A Colonnade in Moonlight. Design for a stage set
143 Lorenzo Sacchetti: A Palace in a Park. Design for a stage set
144 Lorenzo Sacchetti: Antique Ruins. Design for a stage set

INDEX

NAMES OF ARTISTS

Abbate, Niccolò, dell' 7
Albrecht von Sachsen-Teschen 8
Aliense, see Vassilacchi Antonio
Allegri Antonio, see Correggio
Allori, Cristoforo 112
Altdorfer, Albrecht 9
Amigoni, Jacopo 171
Ansaldo, Giovanni Andrea 13, 20, 129, 130
Antonello da Messina 29, 33, 44, 46
Aspetti, Tiziano 88
Assereto, Gioacchino 130
Auwera, Wolfgang van de 154

Baciccia, Giovanni Battista Gaulli 127
Badile, Antonio 84, 85, 86
Balestra, Antonio 136
Bambini, Nicolò 135
Baratta, Pietro 160
Baroccio, Federigo 31, 122
Bartolommeo, Fra 10, 84
Basaiti, Marco 15, 41, 42
Bassano, Jacopo 73, 79, 89, 110, 111
Bassetti, Marcantonio 14, 19, 110, 111
Bastiani, Lazzaro di Jacopo 36
Batoni, Pompeo 171
Battaglioli, Francesco 172
Bazzani, Giuseppe 14, 22, 160, 161, 166
Bedoli, Girolamo (Mazzola) 68
Bega, Cornelisz 69
Bellini, Giovanni 15, 29, 33, 44, 46, 47, 48, 52, 63
Bellotto, Bernardo, called Canaletto 9, 12, 163, 164, 165, 167
Benaglio, Francesco 44
Bencovich, Federico 136, 153, 160
Benso, Giulio 130
Bergamosco, il see Castello Bernardo
Bernardi, Giuseppe, see il Torretto
Bernini, Gianlorenzo 122, 126, 127
Bibiena, Francesco 174
Bibiena, Giuseppe Galli 174
Biscaino, Bartolomeo 20, 130
Blake, William 17

Boccaccino, Boccaccio 64
Boccaccino, Camillo 12, 15, 64, 65, 66, 99, 105
Boltraffio, Giovanni Antonio 43
Bonsignori, Francesco 14, 29, 31, 33, 34, 35
Borcht, Hendrick van der 56, 57
Bordone, Paris 51
Borgianni, Orazio 110
Borgognone, Ambrogio di Stefano 42
Bossi, Antonio 154
Bramantino, Bartolommeo Suardi 42, 45
Brand, Johann Christian 10
Bravo, Cecco 113
Bruegel, Peter (the Elder) 7
Brusaferro, Girolamo 135
Brusasorci, Domenico 84, 86
Brusasorci, Felice 110

Caccia, Guglielmo, called il Moncalvo 18, 50, 101, 102, 103
Caliari, Giuseppe 86
Caliari, Paolo see Veronese
Cambiaso, Luca, called Lucchetto 8, 17, 76, 77, 78, 79, 129
Cambiaso, Orazio 129
Campagnola, Domenico 16, 48, 61, 62, 63, 64, 65
Campagnola, Domenico Follower of 62
Campagnola, Giulio 16, 61, 63
Campi, Bernardino 99, 103, 105
Campi, Giulio 103, 105, 109
Canale, Antonio 20, 163, 164, 165, 166
Canaletto, see Bernardo Bellotto
Canova, Antonio 11, 160
Cantarini, Simone 117
Caravaggio, Michelangelo da 105, 110, 111, 113
Carlotto, see Loth, Johann Carl
Caroto, Giovanni Francesco 84, 86
Carpaccio, Vittore 15, 36, 41, 46
Carpioni, Giulio 12, 19, 117, 118
Carracci, Annibale 9, 10, 103, 126, 133, 171

Carracci, Lodovico 10, 19, 103, 114, 126, 171
Casanova, Francesco 167, 168
Casanova, Giacomo 167
Casanova, Giovanni Battista 167, 168
Castello, Bernardo, called il Bergamosco 13, 76, 78, 79
Castello, Valerio 130
Castiglione, Francesco 128
Castiglione, Giovanni, Benedetto, called Grechetto 10, 20, 122, 125, 126, 127, 128, 129, 130, 169
Cavaliere d'Arpino 105
Celesti, Andrea 131, 132
Cerano, il (Crespi, Giovanni Battista) 103, 105, 109
Cervelli, Francesco 132
Charles III of Spain 153, 156
Cigoli, Lodovico 111
Cima da Conegliano 45
Cimaroli, Giovanni Battista 141
Civerchio, Vincenzo 48
Conca, Sebastiano 49
Cornelis de Wael 113
Correggio, Antonio Allegri 7, 10, 15, 17, 52, 53, 54, 56, 57, 58, 64, 66, 67, 74, 99, 103
Cortona, Pietro da 119, 122, 132
Costa, Lorenzo 52

Delacroix, Eugène 86
Diziani, Gaspare 12, 20, 21, 134, 141, 142, 143, 144, 145, 146, 147, 148, 149, 150, 151, 152, 153, 157, 158
Dorigny, Louis 152
Dürer, Albrecht 7, 9, 76
Dyck, Anthonis van 112, 113, 127, 129, 160

Eissler, Joseph 84
Elsheimer, Adam 111
Esterházy, Family 8
— Miklós, Palatine 8, 9
— Miklós I 8, 9, 168
— Miklós II 9, 10, 11
— Pál 11

Farinati, Paolo 87
Ferdinand I, Habsburg 8
Ferdinand, Archduke of Tyrol 8
Ferramola, Floriano 48
Ferrari, Defendente 101
Ferrari, Francesco Bianchi 52
Ferrari, Gaudenzio 18, 45, 46, 101, 105, 108
Ferrari, Giovanni Andrea de 78, 122
Ferroni, Girolamo 108
Fetti, Domenico 19, 110, 111, 112, 114, 122, 160
Fiammenghino, il see Mauro della Rovere
Fischer, Joseph 10, 11
Flamael, Bertholet 111
Fogolino, Marcello 16, 66, 67
Fontebasso, Francesco 12, 14, 20, 21, 134, 141, 144, 149, 150, 151, 152, 157, 159
Foppa, Vincenzo 42, 48
Fossati, Domenico 175, 176, 177
Francia, Domenico 174
Franceschini, Marcantonio 91
Franco, Giovanni Battista, called "Semolei" 58, 59
Furini, Francesco 112

Galliari, Bernardino 173, 175
Galliari, Fabrizio 23, 173, 174, 175
Gatti, Bernardino, called Soiaro 56, 57, 58
Giambellino, see Bellini, Giovanni
Giampietrino, Pedrini, Giovanni 103
Giordano, Luca 119, 131, 132, 135, 148
Giorgione, Giorgio da Castelfranco 10, 15, 16, 46, 47, 48, 62, 73
Giorgione, Unknown follower of ? about 1530 66
Giorgionesco, Anonymo 16
Giovanni Antonio da Brescia 40
Giovanni, Giuseppe dal Sole 132
Giovanni da San Giovanni 112
Girolamo di Romano, see Romanino
Goltzius, Hendrick 95
Gonzaga, Family 29, 111, 122
— Alfonso 76
— Camillo 76
— Carlo 123, 126
— Maria, Duchess of Mantua 123
Goya, Francisco y Lucientes 148, 153
Grassalkovich, Princess 11
Grassi, Giovannino de' 29
Grechetto, see Castiglione, Giovanni Benedetto
Grimani, Cardinal 83
Grisoni, Giuseppe 142
Guarana, Jacopo 150
Guardi, Francesco 9, 20, 22, 23, 155, 160, 165, 166, 167, 168, 177

Guardi, Giovanni Antonio 131, 166, 167
Guercino 18

Huber, Wolf 9

Jordaens, Jacob 10
Juvarra, Filippo 173, 174

Kern, Anton 21
Kulmbach, Hans von 47

Lanfranco Giovanni 75
Langetti, Giovanni Battista 116, 119
Lanino, Bernardino 101
Lazzarini, Antonio 141
Lazzarini, Gregorio 153
Lelio da Nuovelara, see Orsi, Lelio
Leonardo da Vinci 7, 10, 42, 45, 46, 52,
Liberale da Verona 14, 29, 31, 33, 34
Liberi, Pietro 19, 98, 112, 113, 115, 117, 119, 120, 121,
Ligozzi, Giacomo 129, 130
Lombard master 12, 27, 28
Lorenzini, Giovanni Antonio, Fra 86
Loth, Johann Carl, called Carlotto 14, 19, 115, 116, 117
Loth, Ulrich 115
Lotto, Lorenzo 48, 50
Lucchesi, Matteo 170
Lucchetto, see Luca di Cambiaso
Luini, Bernardo 10, 13, 42, 43, 44, 45
Lys, Jan 114

Maffei, Francesco 88, 117, 160, 166
Maganza, Alessandro 90
Magnasco, Alessandro 9, 132, 163, 166
Malombra, Constantino 62
Malombra, Pietro, 60
Malosso, see Trotti, Giovanni Battista
Mantegna, Andrea 15, 29, 31, 36, 40, 44, 52
Mantegna, Follower of 36, 40
Marcola, Giovanni Battista 134, 135
Marcola, Marco 134, 135
Marieschi, Jacopo 99
Marieschi, Michele 170
Maria Theresa, Habsburg, Empress 8
Mauro della Rovere, Gian 108
Mauro della Rovere, Giovanni Battista, called il Fiammenghino 19, 108, 109, 110
Mazzoni, Sebastiano 19, 112, 113, 119, 132
Mazzuchelli, Pier Francesco, see Morazzone
Mazzuola, Francesco, see Parmigianino
Medici, Family
— Ferdinando II 129, 130
— Giuliano 84
Meldolla, Andrea, see Schiavone
Mengs, Anton Raphael 167, 171
Metz, Conrad Martin 53, 96
Michelangelo Buonarroti 7, 17, 52, 54, 57, 58, 59, 68, 74, 75, 76, 78, 79, 84, 91, 92
Moncalvo, see Caccia, Guglielmo
Montagna, Bartolomeo 15, 16, 44, 45
Morazzone 19, 105, 106, 107, 108, 109
Moretto, Alessandro 61, 84, 86
Morone, Domenico 44

Naldini, Battista 103
Nigretti, Jacopo, see Palma il Giovane
Novelli, Pietro Antonio 8, 23, 171, 172

Orsi, Lelio 9, 14, 17, 74, 75, 76

Padovanino, see Varotari, Alessandro
Pagani, Paolo 119
Paggi, Giovanni Battista 113, 122
Pálffy, Family
— József 9
— Miklós 9
Palladio, Andrea 18, 85, 170
Palma, Antonio 91
Palma il Giovane 8, 14, 18, 61, 89, 90, 91, 92, 93, 94, 95, 96, 97, 99, 104, 110, 114, 115
Palma Vecchio 48, 91
Paltronieri, J. 141
Parmigianino 7, 8, 9, 10, 12, 14, 16, 17, 18, 22, 66, 67, 68, 69, 70, 71, 72, 73, 79, 91, 102, 103, 169
Pellegrini, Giovanni Antonio 9, 20, 21, 131, 132, 133, 134, 136, 141, 144, 145, 146, 147, 148, 153, 157, 162, 166
Perino del Vaga 68, 76
Petrucci, Francesco 86
Philip II, King of Spain 76
Piazzetta, Giovanni Battista 20, 23, 136, 140, 153, 167, 171
Pietro della Vecchia 117
Piola, Pellegrino 130
Piranesi, Giovanni Battista 22, 170, 175
Pisanello (Pisano, Antonio) 15

Pittoni, Francesco 136
Pittoni, Giambattista 20, 21, 136—140, 141, 173
Poccetti, Bernardino 50
Polidoro da Caravaggio 92
Pontormo, Jacopo 10
Pordenone, Giovanni Antonio 50, 57, 61, 64, 66, 79, 99
Poussin, Nicolas 10, 117, 122
Pozzobonelli, Giuseppe 108
Primaticcio, Francesco 7
Procaccini, Camillo 19, 103, 109
Procaccini, Ercole (the Elder) 103
Procaccini, Giulio Cesare 12, 19, 66, 103, 104, 105, 109

Raphael Santi 7, 10, 43, 44, 46, 52, 57, 58, 68, 76, 92, 169
Rembrandt, Harmensz van Rijn 7, 10, 14, 16, 63, 64, 122, 128, 171
Reni, Guido 10, 117, 171
Reynolds, Joshua, Sir 53, 82, 96
Ribera, Jusepe 116, 119
Ricci, Marco 11, 22, 162, 163, 165, 166, 170
Ricci, Sebastiano 9, 20, 21, 119, 131, 132, 133, 134, 135, 136, 141, 144, 152, 153, 157, 162, 163, 166
Rizzi, Stefano 48
Roberti, Ercole 52
Robusti, Jacopo, see Tintoretto
Romanino, Girolamo di Romano 10, 16, 48, 49, 50, 51, 61, 84, 86, 99
Romano, Giulio 58, 64
Rosa, Salvator 163
Rottmayr, Johann Michael 116
Rubens, Peter Paul 7, 22, 86, 112, 113, 126, 129, 160
Rudolph II, Habsburg 8
Ruschi, Francesco 119

Sacchetti, Lorenzo 8, 12, 23, 175, 176, 177
Salimbeni d'Arpuno 105
Salviati, Francesco 103
Saraceni, Carlo 110, 111, 115
Savoldo, Girolamo 48, 50, 86,
Schiavone, called Meldolla, Andrea 62, 73, 79, 99
Schmidt, Joseph 10
Schmutzer, Ferdinand 10
Seiter, Daniel 116
Semino, Andrea 78
Semolei see Franco, Giovanni Battista
Simonini, Francesco 165, 168
Soiaro, see Gatti, Bernardino
Solario, Antonio 43, 103
Spanzotti, Martino 45
Strozzi, Bernardo 19, 20, 112, 113, 114, 115, 122, 129, 160,
Strudel, Peter 92, 93, 116

Tasso, Torquato 78
Tempesta, Antonio 79
Testa, Pietro 117
Tiepolo, Giovanni Battista 9, 12, 20, 22, 86, 122, 132, 153, 154, 155, 156, 157, 160, 170, 172, 173
Tiepolo, Giovanni Domenico 12, 22, 153, 155, 156, 157
Tintoretto, Domenico Robusti 73, 83, 89, 98
Tintoretto, Marietta 84
Tintoretto, Jacopo Robusti 7, 14, 17, 73, 79, 80, 81, 82, 83, 84, 86, 89, 90, 91, 93, 110, 111, 131
Tintoretto, Workshop of 83, 96
Titian 14, 15, 16, 46, 48, 51, 59, 60, 61, 62, 63, 64, 66, 73, 79, 85, 86, 91, 113, 119
Torbido, Francesco 84
Torretti, Giuseppe Bernardi 8, 160
Torretti, Giuseppe 160
Trotti, Giovanni Battista, called Malosso 13, 99, 100, 101

Valeriani, Domenico 137, 170
Valeriani, Giuseppe 137, 170
Varotari, Alessandro 119
Vasari, Giorgio 18, 52, 85, 94
Vassilacchi, Antonio, called Aliense 89, 90, 91
Venetian artist 35
Venetian artist about 1500 40, 41
Venetian artist of the end of the 16th c. 59, 60
Venetian artist about 1600 98, 99
Venetian master from the beginning of the 18th c. 130, 131, 132
Veronese, Bonifazio 73, 79
Veronese, Paolo Caliari 7, 10, 13, 17, 18, 84, 85, 86, 87, 88, 89, 90, 94, 111, 114, 129, 131, 132, 153, 157, 160
Vicentino, Andrea 94, 98, 99

Oxford
— Ashmolean Museum 45, 48, 51, 56, 59, 60, 66, 82, 96, 98, 117, 118, 121, 163, 170
— Christ Church Library 61
— Ince Blundell Hall 56

Padua 36, 52
— Church of San Antonio 164
— Giuseppe Fiocco collection 136
— Museo Civico, Palazzo Conti 36, 98, 121
— Scuola dei SS. Sebastiano e Marco 35
— Theatre of S. Giorgio Crisostomo 175
— Theatre of S. Luca 175
Pannonhalma 119
Paris
— Bibliothèque Nationale 28
— Louvre 20, 48, 54, 56, 60, 66, 68, 74, 81, 140, 141
Parma
— Camera di S. Paolo 57
— Cathedral 53, 68
— Church of San Giovanni Evangelista 53, 54, 68
— Church of Santa Maria della Steccata 16, 17, 68, 69, 70, 71
— Pinacoteca 53
Pavia
— Museo Civico 102
Perugia
— Church of San Pietro 89
Piacenza 18, 57, 99, 105
Poitiers
— Museum 56
Povo by Trento
— Parish church 151
Prague 8, 10
— Národní Galerie 65
Princeton (New Jersey)
— Museum of History of Art 73

Ravenna
— Pinacoteca Civica 113
Rennes
— Musée des Beaux-Arts 52
Rho
— Santuario 105
Rome
— Riva di Trento 91, 136
— Church of S. Silvestro in Capite 105
— Gabinetto Nazionale delle Stampe 82
— Galleria Borghese 111
— Church of Santa Maria dell'Anima 111
Vatican 51, 57
— Sistine Chapel 57
Rotterdam 15
— Museum Boymans-van Beuningen 36, 45, 56
Rovigo 119, 135

Salò 91, 93, 94
Salzburg
— Studienbibliothek 89
Sanpierdarena
— Palazzo Scassi 79
Saronno 45, 46
Siena
— Accademia 93
St. Petersburg, see Leningrad
Süttör, see Eszterháza

Terzo d'Aquileia
— Collection Gino Calligari 131
Tetschen 21
Trento 48, 51, 157, 159
Treviglio
— Church of San Martino 173
Treviso 119, 141, 165
Turin
— Biblioteca Reale 74, 101
— Museo Civico 174
— Teatro Regio 175

Udine 153
— Cappella della Purità 157

Valdagno
— Gaetano Marzotto Collection 136
Varallo
— Sacro Monte 105
Varese 19
— Church of San Vittore 105
— Fondazione Pogliaghi Collection 174
— Sacro Monte 105
Venice 166, 170
— Accademia 41, 94, 98, 115, 133, 136, 172
— Cà Rezzonico 156
— Chiesa di San Rocco 81
— Church of San Fantino 94
— Church of Gesuiti 93

— Church of San Marco 91
— Church of San Salvatore 60
— Church of Sta. Maria del Carmine 18, 96, 97
— Church of Sta. Maria del Giglio 172
— Church of Pietà 157
— Church of S. Stefano 144, 146, 147
— Fondazione Cini 99, 119, 133
— Museo Archeologico 83
— Museo Correr 22, 94, 134, 140, 142, 143, 149, 150, 151, 159
— Oratorio dei Crociferi 91, 97
— Palazzo Ducale 86, 89, 91, 94, 119
Sala del Collegio 86
Sala del Maggior Consiglio 89, 94
— Pinacoteca of S. Lazzaro degli Armeni 173
Vercelli
— Museo Borgogna 46
Verona
— Church of S. Bernardino 31
— Church of S. Fermo Maggiore 31
— Church of Santi Nazzaro e Celso 85
— Church of San Zeno 29, 31
— Museo Civico di Castelvecchio 31, 33, 85
Viadana 66
Vicenza
— Museo Civico 67
— Villa Valmarana 153, 155
Vienna 7, 8, 11, 81
— Albertina 8, 11, 16, 34, 51, 59, 83, 88, 90, 96, 97, 103, 111, 118, 121, 126, 128, 129, 130, 135, 142, 149, 150, 152, 155, 165, 166, 167, 168, 171
— Hoftheater 175, 176
— Kaunitz Palace 10
— Kittsee Palace 168
— Kunsthistorisches Museum 112, 116, 117
— Mariahilf 10
— Nationalbibliothek 35
— Neue Galerie 141, 142
— Palace of the Hungarian Guards 10

Warsaw
— Museum 66, 110
Windsor, Castle 45, 58, 61, 72, 99, 111, 123, 126, 127, 133, 163, 164, 165
Würzburg
— Erzbischöflicher Palast 153, 154